D1144688

U.S. Shipbuilding in the 1970s

U.S. Shipbuilding in the 1970s

William F. Beazer
University of Virginia

William A. Cox
United Nations

Curtis A. Harvey
University of Kentucky

With the Assistance of

Nancy Watkins

Lexington Books
D.C. Heath and Company
Lexington, Massachusetts
Toronto London

Library of Congress Cataloging in Publication Data

Beazer, William F. and Cox, William A. and
Harvey, Curtis A.
U.S. Shipbuilding in the 1970s.
Mass. Lexington Books

Sept. 1972 5-19-72 72-4242

Published simultaneously in Canada.

Printed in the United States of America.

International Standard Book Number: 0-669-74337-1

Library of Congress Catalog Card Number: 72-4242

Contents

List of Figures

List of Tables

Preface

The U.S. shipbuilding industry is unique among major manufacturing industries in the United States. First, it has virtually no customers outside the United States. Second, it has only one major customer inside the country, the U.S. government. As a result, the industry's state of well-being and many of its technological characteristics are primarily a function of past and present government decisions. In this book we attempt to examine the implications of certain kinds of government behavior with respect to U.S. shipyards and to limn the character of potential changes in industry structure and geographical distribution.

No judgments are made about the appropriateness of ship design, the numbers of ships needed, or the timing of these needs. We analyze how illustrative programs may affect commercial-shipbuilding activities. Naval shipyards are excluded from the analysis because they have not built large ships for several years. Our data, provided by a variety of industry and government sources, were current in 1967 and 1968.

Part I examines the productivity and costs of the U.S. shipbuilding industry relative to those of its major international competitors. It provides estimates of the degree to which the industry is unable to compete internationally and indicates why the United States has become a closed system with essentially one buyer, the U.S. government.

Part II then describes the method of analysis and the use of data. The selection of the 15 private shipyards included and the grouping of ship types are discussed in Chapter 2. Chapter 3 describes the production side of shipbuilding, outlining the current capital and labor resources in the yards and the techniques of employing these resources to build ships. Included is a discussion of recent and potential technological changes in the industry and estimates of the productivity increases which they make possible.

Chapter 4 contains a description of shipyard cost functions and their parameters. The costs are those encountered by the shipyards only and do not include such additional components as the manufacturing cost of shipboard systems which are only installed by the shipyard.[1] A price is calculated for each ship type built at each yard as a function of the first-ship cost and the number of ships of that type which the yard can build.

In Part III we analyze the results of matching two forecasts of demand for U.S.-built naval and merchant ships against existing and modernized shipbuilding capacity. The results include:

1. *Least-cost distributions of ship orders* among yards and costal regions of the United States.
2. Expected *additions to the labor force* in response to different programs.

3. Expected *investments* in equipment modernization and in new shipyards.
4. Effects on *ship prices* of variations in demand and investment.
5. The *magnitude of unutilized capacity* in the industry and the probable number of firms remaining in or dropping out.
6. The costs and other implications of *dispersing the orders* among all yards to maintain excess capacity as a "mobilization base."

Chapter 6 discusses the implications of these first five points for the smaller of the two shipbuilding programs with delivery schedules peaked in the early 1970s. Chapter 7 compares these results with those for the larger program with similar timing of delivery requirements. The effects of a smoother production and delivery schedule on both program levels are then tested in Chapter 8.

The maintenance of excess shipbuilding capacity in the industry is analyzed in Chapter 9. These results include the cost of such a policy and its effect on allocation of orders and investment in new equipment, especially as they differ from the results discussed in Chapters 6 and 7. Chapter 10 examines the potential profitability of one or more entirely new shipyards and the effects these yards would have on the prices of ships and replacement investment in existing yards. Finally, Chapter 11 summarizes the results of Part III. The remainder of the book contains appendixes.

The research for the book was accomplished at the Institute for Defense Analyses under a contract with the Office of Systems Analysis in the U.S. Department of Defense. Nothing contained herein, however, should be construed as the official view of any of these organizations. In order to obtain data that the shipyards considered proprietary, it was agreed that the identity of individual yards would not be disclosed.

We have a number of debts to acknowledge. The first is to Harry Williams, John Wells, Elizabeth Johnston, and Edward Sanders for permission to borrow extensively from their study of international productivity differences in shipbuilding, "An Economic Analysis of U.S. Naval Shipbuilding Costs," IDA Report R-120. Most of the data in Chapter 1 were obtained from this source. The second major debt is to Jane Leavitt who played a principal role in transforming the original study into its present form. No less important were the patience and skill of Evelyn Cole and Dorothy Mendonsa. Their extraordinary efforts greatly lightened the burden of producing the final manuscript and the many drafts that came before it.

We also wish to thank several colleagues for the many helpful suggestions on various phases of the Report, in particular Harry Williams, William Niskanen, and Leonard Bates. In addition, the patient counseling of people in the U.S. Department of Defense, the Naval Ship Systems Command, the Navy Shipyard Modernization Office and the Shipbuilders Council of America contributed greatly to making the study possible. Finally, managers and employees of U.S. and foreign shipyards and of shipbuilding equipment manufacturers provided the researchers with a wide range of valuable information vital to the successful conclusion of the study.

Part I
Historical Perspectives

1 U.S. Shipbuilding Industry: Productivity and Markets

The U.S. shipbuilding industry reached a peak of ship production at the end of World War II, having built 5,777 ships during the war. Fifty-seven major private shipyards were in operation—23 on the East Coast, 22 on the West, and 12 on the Gulf. In addition to achieving high production levels, these yards were innovative and brought new concepts to the industry, notably multiple production of standardized designs, such as the *Victory Ship*, a switch from riveted to welded shipbuilding, and techniques for prefabricating large subassemblies. These new ideas and processes were later adopted by Japanese and European shipbuilders.

Since then, the number of major U.S. shipyards has dropped from 57 to 15. Employment has declined 80 percent, while the industry's volume of business in deflated dollars has dropped proportionately. To compound the problem, the industry has suffered from wide fluctuations of demand over the entire postwar period. For example, between the years 1947 and 1949 the number of ships built were 19, 75, and 5, respectively. The years 1950 to 1952 show 16, 77, and 27 ships each. Between 1955 and 1957, 18, 68, and 35 ships were built.[1] The demand was widely spread with a relatively small number of ships (usually two to four) built in each yard during a year. The same kind of pattern has continued to the present.

In an effort to maintain a certain number of yards operating, the government has parcelled out its orders among several yards, rather than giving a single yard the entire run of a specific ship. In effect, this has put shipbuilders in the position of contractors, building small numbers of ships to individual specifications, rather than manufacturers producing large quantities of identical items. They are unable to profit from learning curve benefits which accrue with long runs. While keeping these yards alive, this government action kills incentive and competition. The government subsidies which support the industry pay for a small number of expensive vessels, while the manner in which orders are given discourages capital investment and expansion of yards. These procurement policies, coupled with the uncertain demand, help to perpetuate risk-aversion techniques which do not minimize costs for the industry.

The inherent instability of the market and the small orders on which ships have been bought have induced the industry to adopt many risk-aversion techniques, which lower a yard's efficiency yet compensate for unstable demand. The most pervasive is the choice of a production process that involves a high ratio of labor to capital, making the industry more labor-intensive than would be optimal under stable market conditions. Comparisons with other domestic industries and with foreign shipbuilders can give some indication of the degree of labor-intensiveness in U.S. shipbuilding.

1-1 Differences in Production Techniques in U.S. and Foreign Shipbuilding

In the following sections we examine some evidence that the significant differential between U.S. and foreign production costs can be attributed to greater labor productivity and more capital-intensive production techniques in Sweden and Japan. An attempt is made to identify some valid and empirically verifiable indicators of differences in production processes in ship manufacture and to compare U.S. shipbuilding with (1) other U.S. manufacturing industries and (2) the shipbuilding industries in foreign countries.

Whether or not one technique is more "efficient" than another depends upon the nature of the demand to be satisfied. Efficient production of unique items to special order may call for a much more labor-intensive production technique than the efficient manufacture of large numbers of identical items. Thus, efficiency and capital intensiveness cannot be equated nor can the capital-labor ratio be used as some kind of surrogate measure of efficiency, unless one first defines the nature of the demand. If the relative prices of capital and labor are the same in two countries but one observes considerably different capital labor ratios in the same industry in both, then the most one can postulate with any assurance is that different production techniques are being used. If the differences in ratios persist over time, a further possible deduction is that the industry is geared to a different set of demand conditions in each country. Neither industry may be efficient for the demand conditions facing the other but each may be efficient for its own.

Much the same conclusions can be drawn, although perhaps more tentatively, for different industries within the same country. Where product characteristics and the relative unit costs of labor and capital are comparable, the presence of different capital/labor ratios indicates different production techniques are being used. These different techniques most probably derive from different demand structures.

An examination of factor proportions used in producing similar products can be useful in identifying and categorizing industries according to production technique. The composition of factors used in an industry in one country can also be compared with factor proportions used in the same industry in other countries. Where dissimilar usage between industries and between countries is found, an examination of the reasons for the differential can prove helpful and can perhaps provide some insight into the effects on the organization of the industry of differences in the market structure.

Factor Composition

If the unit prices of capital and labor are approximately the same to all manufacturing industries, the proportion of factors of production used in an industry may be indicative of the nature of the market structure and may be a measure of the degree of standardization output and mechanization of the production process that the demand characteristics permit. Indices of capital-labor ratios for several U.S. industries are shown in Table 1-1. The ratio for shipbuilding is the lowest in every period. The fact that the shipbuilding industry uses higher proportions of labor than any of the other industries shown in the table does not prove that shipbuilding is inefficient nor that the ship market is any different from that for the other industries. It could be that efficient shipbuilding technology is simply very labor-intensive.

The indices of capital-labor ratios for Sweden in Table 1-2, however, suggest that shipbuilding is not more labor-intensive than other manufacturing industries. The indices for the Swedish shipbuilding industry show that, although the industry was relatively labor-intensive in 1958, by 1963 its capital-labor ratio was near the *all industry* average and above the *all metal and engineering industry* average. It is also relevant that in 1963 the Swedish average for all industries was not significantly different from the U.S. average.

The figures in Table 1-1 indicate that although the capital-labor ratio for shipbuilding in the United States has increased at about the same rate as the average for *all manufacturing*, the gap between the U.S. shipbuilding industry and other industries has not diminished over time. The Swedish situation was quite different. The ratio increased more rapidly for the shipbuilding industry than for others, and the gap was narrowed to insignificance. It would appear through this comparison of U.S. and Swedish capital-labor indices that shipbuilding is not inherently more labor-intensive than other related industries. Therefore, it is possible to interpret the low capital-labor ratios in U.S. shipbuilding as an indication that U.S. shipbuilding involves different technology from the Swedish and, as a corollary, that the markets they build for are not the same. An industry comparison of new capital expenditures and employment can shed light on how reliable an indicator it is.

New Capital Expenditures and Employment

Capital-labor ratios can increase if either of the two factors changes relative to the other. A rise does not necessarily imply an absolute increase in capital expenditures. The tables and figures in this section help to show what lies behind the changes in the ratios that have occurred, by examining separately the changes in capital and labor.

The employment figures in Table 1-3 show that from 1958 through 1964, with the exception of the *aircraft* industry, most industries in the U.S. similar to shipbuilding had relatively stable or slightly increasing employment levels. Over the same period, new capital expenditures were generally increasing in all but the *shipbuilding and repairing* industry and the *fabricated metal products* industry. The capital expenditures are graphed in Figure 1-1.

Investment on a per employee and per production worker basis appears in Table 1-4 and Figure 1-2. Per capita investment in the *shipbuilding and repairing* industry declined because real new capital expenditures fell while employment remained stable. The same thing was true in the *fabricated metal products*

Table 1-1
Approximate Capital-Labor Ratio Indices in U.S. Manufacturing Industries*

Year	All Manufacturing Industries	Durable-goods Industries	Shipbuilding and Repairing (SIC 3731)	Fabricated Metal Products (SIC 3411)	Aircraft (SIC 3721)	Motor Vehicles and Parts (SIC 3717)
1958	n.a.	n.a.	0.36	0.76	0.45	1.10
1959	n.a.	n.a.	0.42	0.54	0.44	1.47
1960	n.a.	n.a.	0.38	0.47	0.59	1.63
1961	1.05	0.93	0.40	0.58	0.58	1.66
1962	1.19	0.91	0.48	0.53	0.63	2.05
1963	1.32	1.06	0.52	0.61	0.84	2.34
1964	1.38	1.33	0.58	0.78	0.92	2.44

*The capital-labor ratio indices are approximations of the capital-labor ratios, not the exact ratios. The method for determining these ratios is discussed in Appendix A of H. Williams, et al.

Source: H. Williams, et al., "An Economic Analysis of U.S. Naval Shipbuilding Costs," IDA, December 1966, p. 7.

Table 1-2
Approximate Capital-Labor Ratio Indices in Swedish Manufacturing Industries

Year	All Manufacturing Industries	All Metal and Engineering Industries	Shipyards and Boat Building	Iron and Steel Works	Transportation Equipment Other Than Ships and Boats
1958	0.85	0.58	0.46	0.91	0.48
1959	1.01	0.68	0.50	1.11	0.70
1960	1.09	0.66	0.63	1.41	0.79
1961	1.08	0.74	0.60	1.60	0.74
1962	1.13	0.92	1.01	1.36	0.94
1963	1.24	1.04	1.16	1.26	1.04

Source: H. Williams, et al., p. 8.

Table 1-3
Real New Capital Expenditures, Total Employees, and Number of Production Workers in Selected U.S. Manufacturing Industries, 1958 to 1964

Year	All Manufacturing Industries	Duable-goods Industries	Shipbuilding and Repairing (SIC 3731)	Fabricated Metal Products (SIC 3441)	Aircraft (SIC 3721)	Motor Vehicles and Parts (SIC 3717)
		Real New Capital Expenditures (millions)*				
1958	9,593	4,731	39	38	94	334
1959	8,628	4,515	33	27	87	379
1960	9,854	5,214	28	26	60	452
1961	9,564	4,764	30	24	69	374
1962	10,190	5,123	22	19	115	481
1963	10,976	5,896	23	27	110	628
1964	13,032	7,050	31	36	97	888
		Total Number of Employees (thousands)				
1958	15,422	8,538	119	91	378	546
1959	16,059	9,001	116	83	369	600
1960	16,160	9,092	108	88	302	658
1961	15,728	8,780	114	84	305	570
1962	16,163	9,157	112	79	326	628
1963	16,238	9,228	114	86	302	649
1964	16,497	9,407	115	87	284	690
		Total Number of Production Workers (thousands)				
1958	11,666	6,449	101	68	251	434
1959	12,265	6,881	96	60	226	489
1960	12,212	6,851	90	64	178	541
1961	11,778	6,533	96	62	173	460
1962	12,130	6,841	94	59	180	517
1963	12,216	6,913	96	64	166	535
1964	12,431	7,076	97	65	160	569

*In 1958 constant dollars.

Source: H. Williams, et al., p. 8.

industry. The *all manufacturing, durable-goods*, and *motor vehicles and parts* industries experienced increases in real new capital expenditures per employee and per production worker because real new capital expenditures increased at a faster rate than employment. The *aircraft* industry had a surge of new investment during 1962 and 1963, while employment declined.

These data tend to support the hypothesis that the U.S. shipbuilding industry has changed its technology less rapidly than others. On the average, up until the

Table 1-4
Real New Capital Expenditures per Employee and per Production Worker in Selected U.S. Manufacturing Industries, 1958 to 1964*

Year	All Manufacturing Industries	Durable-goods Industries	Shipbuilding and Repairing (SIC 3731)	Fabricated Metal Products (SIC 3441)	Aircraft (SIC 3721)	Motor Vehicles and Parts (SIC 3717)
	Real New Capital Expenditures Per Employee, $					
1958	622	554	325	413	250	612
1959	537	502	280	332	235	632
1960	610	574	257	297	199	687
1961	608	543	267	288	226	656
1962	630	559	199	234	353	766
1963	676	639	203	316	365	967
1964	790	749	270	410	343	1,287
	Real New Capital Expenditures Per Production Worker, $					
1958	822	734	383	554	375	770
1959	703	656	339	459	384	774
1960	807	761	307	408	338	837
1961	812	729	318	389	400	812
1962	840	749	236	314	639	930
1963	898	853	242	425	662	1,173
1964	1,048	996	320	551	610	1,560

*Figures derived from Table 1-3.
Source: H. Williams, et al., p. 14.

mid-1960s, other industries in the United States were substituting capital for labor at a faster rate than the *shipbuilding and repairing* industry.

A similar analysis can be made of Sweden's industries. Table 1-5 and Figure 1-3 indicate that employment from 1958 to 1963 remained relatively constant in Swedish shipyards, while real new capital investment experienced two surges (1958 and 1961 to 1962). The increase in real new capital expenditures per employee and per production worker shown in Table 1-6 and Figure 1-4 was the result of heavy capital expenditures in the shipbuilding industry. Clearly, Swedish shipbuilding has had a much greater degree of substitution of capital for labor than the U.S. shipbuilding industry.

Thus, there is clear evidence that the capital-labor ratios in the U.S. shipbuilding and repairing industry are lower than those in other U.S. manufacturing industries, and the U.S. ratios have not increased as rapidly as those in Sweden. The capital-labor ratios and the investment behavior of Sweden strongly suggest that capital *can* be substituted for labor in shipbuilding just as in other industries. The next section indicates what the effect of this substitution could be.

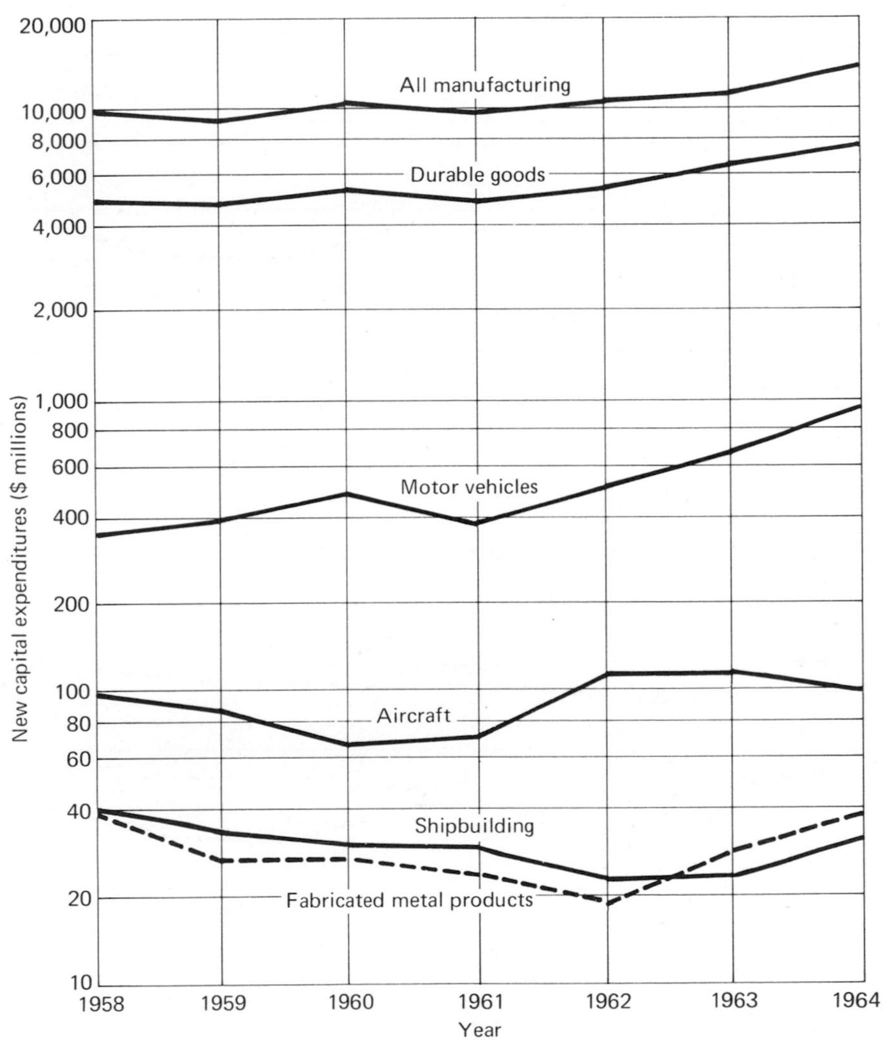

Figure 1-1. Real new capital expenditures in U.S. manufacturing industries. From H. Williams, et al., p. 14.

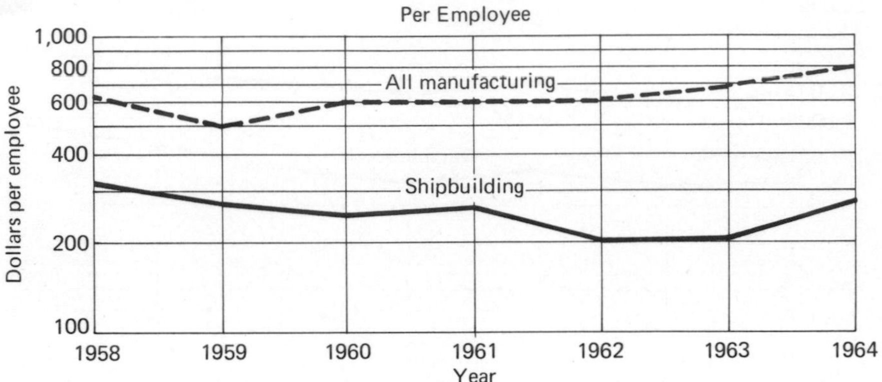

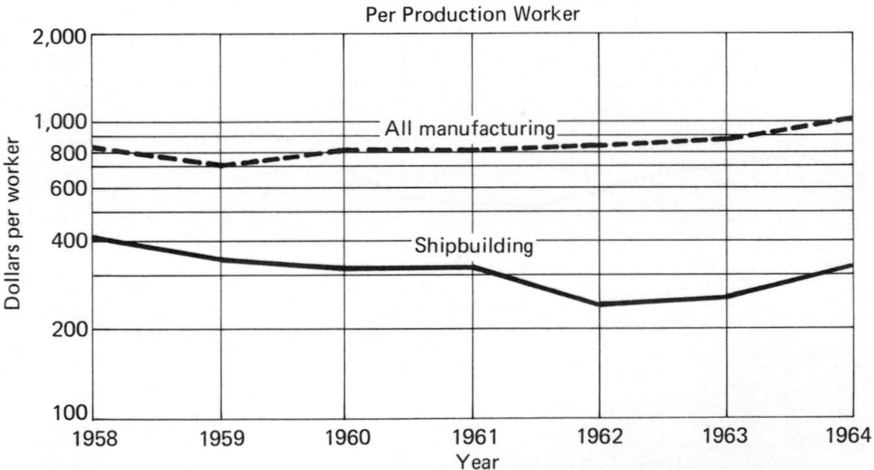

Figure 1-2. Real new capital expenditures in United States. From H. Williams, et al., p. 14.

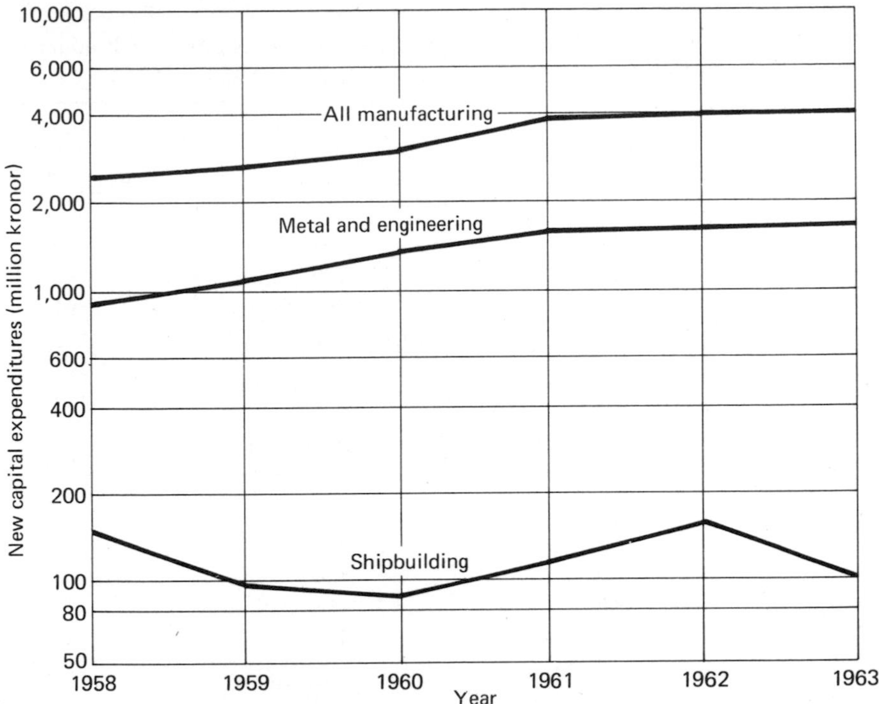

Figure 1–3. Real new capital expenditures in Swedish manufacturing industries. From H. Williams, et al., p. 18.

Differences in Labor Productivity[2]

Differences in labor productivity between countries are difficult to measure, but the data presented below indicate that for shipbuilding a considerable gap exists between the United States and other countries. Table 1-7 presents estimates of average man-hours per steel-weight ton for merchant ships in the United States, Sweden, United Kingdom, and Japan. The six-year averages indicate that man-hours per steel-weight ton in the United States have been roughly double those in Sweden and Japan. Stated another way, productivity in the United States has been roughly one-half that of Sweden and Japan. Table 1-8 shows the differences in hourly labor cost per production worker. Other things equal, the data on labor cost suggest that to be competitive, the United States should have the highest labor productivity, followed by Sweden, the United Kingdom, and Japan. In actuality, Japan moved to the top position, and the United States and United Kingdom were competing for fourth place.

Table 1-5
Real New Capital Expenditures, Total Employees, and Number of Production Workers in Selected Swedish Manufacturing Industries, 1958 to 1963

Year	All Manufacturing Industries	All Metal and Engineering Industries	Shipyards and Boat Building
	Real New Capital Expenditures (million kronor)		
1958	2,483	965	149
1959	2,737	1,100	98
1960	3,218	1,369	91
1961	3,925	1,632	115
1962	4,054	1,623	165
1963	4,120	1,749	103
	Total Number of Employees (thousands)		
1958	841	392	35
1959	850	399	33
1960	896	428	32
1961	930	456	33
1962	940	468	34
1963	939	467	32
	Number of Production Workers (thousands)		
1958	661	296	28
1959	665	299	26
1960	699	321	25
1961	719	339	26
1962	718	344	26
1963	711	339	25

Source: H. Williams, et al., p. 13.

Demand, Production Techniques and Efficiency

The purpose of the foregoing analysis has been to determine whether the available economic data indicate that, foreign and U.S. shipyards use different technology. The capital-labor ratio indices in U.S. shipbuilding are much lower than the average for all manufacturing industries. The data for the Swedish shipbuilding industry demonstrate that low capital-labor ratios are not a necessary characteristic of a shipbuilding industry. The new capital expenditure figures indicate that investment in the U.S. shipbuilding industry has not increased as rapidly as other U.S. industries and certainly not as rapidly as the shipbuilding industries in Sweden and Japan. There appear to be clear-cut international differences in productivity in commercial shipbuilding. Since

Table 1-6
Real New Capital Expenditures Per Employee and Per Production Worker in Selected Swedish Industries, 1958 to 1963* (Swedish kronor)

Year	All Manufacturing Industries	All Metals and Engineering Industries	Shipyards and Boat Building
	Real New Capital Expenditures Per Employee		
1958	2952	2460	4294
1959	3219	2757	3009
1960	3593	3197	2814
1961	4219	3578	3444
1962	4313	3468	4896
1963	4388	3744	3183
	Real New Capital Expenditures Per Production Worker		
1958	3755	3257	5373
1959	4115	3674	3827
1960	4606	4262	3671
1961	5458	4813	4454
1962	5644	4722	6380
1963	5794	5158	4202

*Figures derived from Table 1-5.
Source: H. Williams, et al., p. 20.

factor-price ratios do not account for the differences, it is apparent that U.S. shipbuilding does use a different technology from its foreign competitors. It also seems clear that the choice of technology does not permit the U.S. industry to compete internationally. Whether the U.S. shipbuilders have been inefficient over the short run is another matter. Given their economic environment, they actually may have been operating at least-cost positions.

If one assumes that firms behave like profit maximizers, what appears to be inefficient behavior may well be optimal for the short run, given the market situation. If the market situation continues over a series of short runs, such behavior becomes optimal for individual firms over the long run as well. The firms' production decisions may, nevertheless, be inefficient relative to what they could be since they are partially a function of the way in which demand is allocated. If the demand is generated in a competitive market, the supply response must be considered optimal because nothing can be done to affect demand. If the demand characteristics are policy-determined, however, as they are for U.S. Naval and Merchant ships, and they deviate from a competitive market, the supply response can be inefficient relative to what it could be. To call the supply response inefficient, however, is to place the blame in the wrong place. What we should say is that the demand is allocated inefficiently. In the following pages we examine how the demand characteristics affect supply.

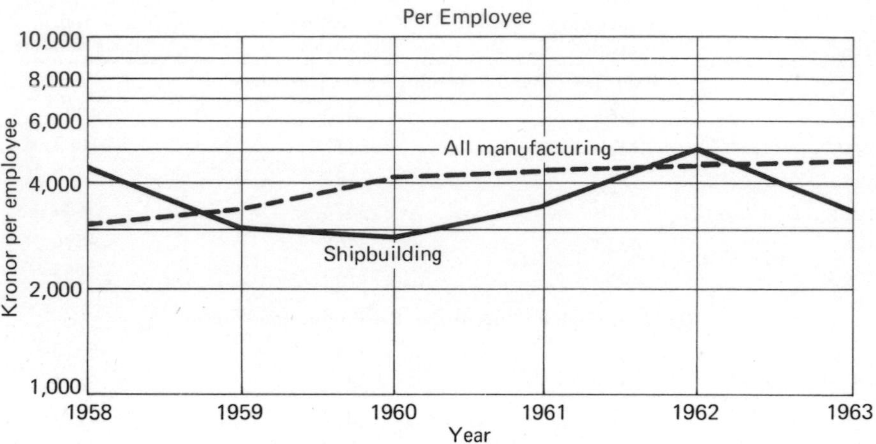

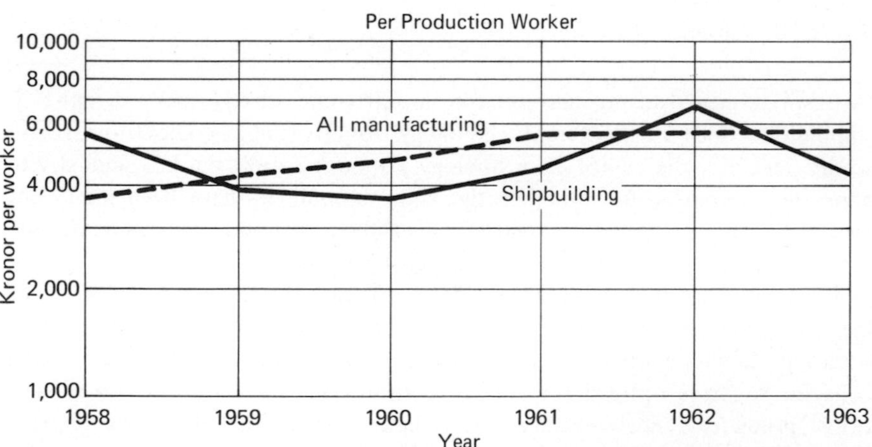

Figure 1–4. Real new capital expenditures in Sweden. H. Williams, et al., p. 19.

Table 1-7
Labor Productivity for Merchant-ship Construction, Selected Countries, 1960 to 1965

Country	1960	1961	1962	1963	1964	1965	Six-year Average
			Man-hours Per Steel-weight Ton*				
United States	221	157	124	124	202	220	164
United Kingdom	218	206	223	151	180	140	187
Sweden	102	98	84	75	82	62	82
Japan	109	104	76	77	62	39	70
			Relative Productivity (Sweden = 100)				
Sweden	100	100	100	100	100	100	100
Japan	94	94	111	97	132	159	117
United States	46	62	68	60	41	28	50
United Kingdom	47	48	38	50	45	44	44

*The man-hours are total direct man-hours including outfitting man-hours.
Source: H. Williams, et al., p. 22.

Table 1-8
Average Hourly Earnings of Production Workers* in Shipbuilding Industries of Selected Countries

Year	United States	Sweden	United Kingdom	Japan
		U.S. Dollars		
1960	3.19	1.49	0.89	0.68
1961	3.33	1.50	0.95	0.72
1962	3.41	1.69	0.96	0.73
1963	3.47	1.83	1.01	0.81
1964	3.53	1.98	1.08	0.90
1965	3.53	2.13	1.18	0.93
		Percent of U.S. Hourly Earnings		
1960	100	46	28	21
1961	100	45	29	22
1962	100	50	28	21
1963	100	53	29	23
1964	100	56	31	25
1965	100	60	33	26

*Includes all wage payments, overtime, bonuses, welfare funds, employer contributions, etc. Figures do not account for differences in purchasing power.
Source: H. Williams, et al., p. 23.

1-2 The U.S. Ship Market: Uncertainty and Procurement Policies

Largely as a result of the inability of U.S. shipyards to compete internationally, the buyer-seller relationships in the United States are different from those in foreign commercial and naval ship markets. Foreign shipbuilders react to impersonal market forces. In contrast, American producers must be responsive to the conditions set up by a singler buyer—the U.S. government.[3] Primarily as a result of government procurement practices, firms have been inclined to take a passive attitude toward innovation.

As a monopsonist, the government has virtually complete control over the product and market conditions shipbuilders face. Thus it could create a market structure similar to that found in the world competitive market. The size of the market for U.S. ship manufacture is comparable in dollar value with the world market for commercial and naval ships. Private shipyard newbuilding and the potential size of single buys of the same type of ship are both large enough to ensure that rational and efficient demand schedules are possible.[4]

A commercial ship-owner buying a large number of ships would certainly order them all from a single yard in order to be able to obtain the lowest possible price through purchasing in volume. The U.S. Government should have the same incentives, but it has responded in quite a different way. Government procurement practices since the end of World War II have permitted U.S. shipbuilders to bid only on small numbers of ships at any one time. Through 1965, no private yard had an opportunity to bid on more than seven units of a particular kind of ship, and even this large a number occurred only in the case of the SSBNs and DEs. Table 1-9 presents procurement data on some of the major ship programs between 1951 and 1965. During the five-year period 1957 to 1961, the government actually procured 23 DDGs. Although this ship program could have been offered as a single package, it was contracted out to six different shipyards. By scanning down the *number procured* column, one can see that in all cases there were opportunities to obtain the benefits of high dollar and unit volume. Total demand could have been structured so that year-to-year uncertainty would have been reduced for individual firms.

This fragmentation of orders virtually eliminated incentives for innovation and reorganization of production techniques. In addition, these small orders were spread throughout the industry, presumably in the belief that maintaining a number of shipyards in business is the optimal way to be sure of having an adequate mobilization base should one be needed. Under these market conditions, excess capacity in the form of old capital equipment has characterized the industry. The mobilization policy has been based on the implicit premise that mobilization is best accomplished with obsolete technology.

A fairly typical case of U.S. naval-ship procurement practice over a 15-year period is illustrated in Table 1-10.[5] During this time, the government bought 55

Table 1-9
Possible Five-year Procurement Programs for Selected Ships and Actual Government Procurement Practice*

			Actual Procurement Practice		
Type of Ship	Period (Dates)	Number Procured	Number of Shipyards Involved	Maximum to Single Shipyard	Average to Single Shipyard
DD	1953-1957	18	4	9	5
DDG	1957-1961	23	6	6	4
DLG	1956-1960	19	8	5	2
SSBN	1961-1965	32	4	13	8
SSN	1956-1960	23	7	5	3
SSN	1961-1965	23	7	6	3
LST	1952-1956	22	7	5	3
DE	1953-1957	16	6	4	3
DE	1961-1965	36	6	10	6

destroyer escorts. Eight different shipyards were involved. Until 1964 no shipyard had an order of more than four ships. In the three years when fairly large numbers of ships were involved (1955, 1964, and 1965), orders were distributed among at least three yards in each case. Clearly, no firm could plan on a large production run; nor was there a high degree of certainty that the firm would win a follow-on contract to sustain production. Under these circumstances firms had little or no opportunity to explore possible economies of scale with respect to producing destroyer escorts, and they apparently had little or no control over the rate of production. Furthermore, the distribution of orders over time and among yards reduced the possibility of cost savings from learning.

This process of fragmenting orders and thereby creating great variability and uncertainty in the market for naval ships appears to have contributed to the low capital-labor ratios discussed earlier. To survive under the market conditions posed, any firm will engage in risk-averting practices, such as the use of more labor-intensive production methods. Given predictable, stable market conditions, a firm will use that combination of capital and labor which is most efficient relative to its output. When demand increases and the increase is expected to continue, the firm would adjust its factor proportions optimally. But in cases where demand is uncertain and unstable, a firm would sensibly opt to satisfy a demand increase solely by increasing its labor force, since labor can be layed off but capital expansion costs are permanent. This decision rule, which is perfectly defensible for the individual shipyard, is nevertheless uneconomic from an overall point of view and will inevitably increase the unit cost of production relative to what it would be under an optimal system of allocating demand.

The government's fragmentation of orders resulted in several firms producing

Table 1-10
Government Procurement of Destroyer Escorts from Private Yards*

Shipyard	1951	1952	1953	1954	1955	1956	1957	1958	1959	1960	1961	1962	1963	1964	1965	1951-1965 Total
Avondale						2	2			2		3		3	3	16
Bath		1	2													3
Bethlehem, San Francisco					2						2					4
Defoe				2									3			5
New York Ship					4											4
Lockheed					2								2	1	4	9
Todd, San Pedro														3	4	7
Todd, Seattle														3	4	7
Total, all yards		1	2	2	8	2	2			2	2	3	5	10	15	55
Possible five-year program					17							38				

*See Appendix B, H. Williams, for source of data.

Source: H. Williams, et al., p. 37.

diverse products rather than specializing. There is, of course, some similarity of product within various ship types, e.g., destroyers, but this is not equivalent to building a large number of ships of the same class. It cannot be maintained that a yard should specialize only in a single class of ships. However, the dollar and unit volume of each ship buy should, if possible, be large enough to take ample advantage of volume and rate economies regardless of whether the firm is producing other ship types.

1-3 U.S. Shipbuilding: A Closed System

The malaise that has characterized the shipbuilding industry has tended to feed upon and be reinforced by the government policies that were meant to combat it. As the U.S. shipbuilding industry became less able to compete in world markets, the navy through its procurement policies attempted to maintain yards in business by spreading orders across several different yards rather than place sizeable orders with one. Construction techniques aimed at producing large numbers of identical ships have little value if an order is likely to amount to three or four ships at the most. Thus, yards found it easier to ignore the loss of world markets as long as they were relatively sure of participating in government-financed construction without making large capital expenditures or attempting to modernize facilities. As a result, the gap between foreign and domestic shipyard productivity has widened over time.

In our analysis of the U.S. industry, we make no further reference to international relationships. The major buyer, the U.S. government, is prevented from buying elsewhere, and international markets are effectively foreclosed to the producers because of their high costs.[6] Thus, the U.S. ship market is a closed system which operates in nearly complete independence from the rest of the world.

We do make one significant break with the past, however. Rather than concede that the historical procedures in ship allocation provide the best predictions of the future, we analyze the industry and its responses to different simulated levels of demand under the optimistic assumption that orders for naval and merchant ships will be allocated as though the U.S. government were attempting to minimize its procurement costs. Starting from this basis we then examine the cost of departure from optimal procurement policies.

Part II provides a description of the industry and the projected ship demands that might approximate its production. It also outlines the mathematical model used to examine the industry's response to the different demand levels and procurement policies.

Part II
Method of Analysis and Processing of Data

2 Shipyards, Demand Levels, and Ship Categories

2-1 The Selection of Shipyards

Even with a very large model, analyzing in detail the entire U.S. shipbuilding industry would be impossible. Our main interest, moreover, is only those private shipyards that have built large oceangoing ships (exceeding 300 feet in length) in the past decade or have retained a capability and interest in doing so. Table 2-1 lists the 15 yards meeting this criterion and indicates the types of ships that each yard can build. Yards are ordered in the list by the number of their building positions. Four of these yards (including Litton) are on the Gulf Coast, six are on the East Coast, and four are in the West. One yard is on Lake Huron.

The construction capabilities of each yard are also listed in the table. For instance, only three yards, Newport News, Quincy, and Litton, have the experience and the facilities to build ships of all types and sizes; only four yards can build nuclear submarines, and so forth. The number and kinds of building positions are shown in the second column.

2-2 Ship Demand

Because the demand for both naval and merchant ships is uncertain and difficult to forecast, the implications of two substantially different shipbuilding programs, one considerably larger than the other, were examined. The smaller of the two programs is based on the 1968 Five-Year Financial Plan for naval-ship construction, modified by a conservative replacement policy for fleet ships superannuated in the period after 1973. An annual average of 36 ships of various types would be bought. This number includes a modest destroyer construction program and incorporates no new destroyer design beyond the DD-943 class. No fast-deployment logistics ships (FDLs) and only those submarines currently in production are included. For merchant ships, a construction rate of 20 ships per year is projected. Included in this number are 11 federally subsidized cargo liners and container ships[1] and 9 dry cargo ships and tankers for service in U.S. coastal commerce and the Military Sea Transport Service (MSTS) fleet. It was assumed that U.S. yards would not win contracts to build foreign-flag ships and that U.S.-flag operators would not win permission to buy abroad.

The larger shipbuilding program, comprising an annual average of 69 ships, includes about 30 percent more destroyers, 30 FDLs or their equivalent, a new

Table 2-1
Size and Capabilities of Shipyards Included in This Study

Shipyard	No. of Building Positions*	Shipbuilding Capabilities†
Newport News Shipbuilding	7 Slipways 3 Graving docks	All types and sizes, including submarines and nuclear
Bethlehem Steel, Sparrows Point	10 Slipways	Commercial and noncombatant naval surface ships, nonnuclear; up to 900 ft.
Ingalls Shipbuilding	10 Slipways	Commercial and naval surface ships and submarines, including nuclear, up to 700 ft.
General Dynamics Groton	6 Active slipways 2 Graving docks	Submarines, including nuclear
General Dynamics Quincy Yard	3 Slipways 3 Graving docks	All types and sizes, including submarines and nuclear
Bath Iron Works	5 Slipways	Commercial and nonnuclear surface ships up to 700 ft.
Alabama Dry Dock	5 Slipways	Naval noncombatants up to 620 ft.
National Steel and Shipbuilding	4 Slipways	Commercial and nonnuclear, noncombatant naval surface ships up to 750 ft.
Sun Shipbuilding	4 Slipways	Commercial ships, all sizes
Lockheed Shipbuilding	3 Slipways	Commercial and nonnuclear naval surface ships up to 600 ft.
Todd, San Pedro	3 Slipways	Commercial and nonnuclear naval surface ships up to 600 ft.
Todd, Seattle	2 Slipways	Commercial and nonnuclear naval surface ships up to 550 ft.
Avondale	2 Side-launch facilities	Commercial and nonnuclear naval surface ships up to 600 ft.
Defoe Shipbuilding	2 Slide-launch facilities	Commercial and nonnuclear naval surface ships up to 600 ft.
Litton, Pascagoula	1 Elevator facility	All types and sizes

*Numbers include some dry docks devoted to repair work.

†Capabilities are determined from size of building positions and from past activities. Most yards are assumed capable of building commercial ships within their size limits even though they have no recent history of doing so.

submarine program beginning in the late 1970s, a doubled merchant ship replacement effort under federal subsidy, and greatly increased unsubsidized merchant marine and tanker construction. The additions to naval procurement amount to 45 percent more ships than in the smaller program, while the demand for merchant ships is increased by 135 percent. Merchant ships in this program comprise 68 percent of the total number, compared with 57 percent in the smaller program.[2]

Both programs were tested under two assumptions about the timing of orders: (1) cumulative requirements specified for each four-year time period, with peak production rates in the early periods, and (2) a total fleet requirement specified at the end of the third period only. In the second case, the delivery schedule is one that yields not only a minimum cost distribution of contracts but also a production rate which minimizes resource inputs. (See Chapter 8.)

2-3 Combining Ships into Categories

In order to make the analytical problem more manageable, the 15 to 17 ship design classes dealt with were consolidated into a smaller number of ship categories representing shipbuilding "activities." Consolidation was accomplished by combining into one shipbuilding activity different ships requiring similar proportions of raw material and of the labor skills that are in restricted supply.[3] Using the initial assumption that ships with similar functions have similar input proportions, the 10 to 12 design classes of naval ships were grouped into five functional categories. Naval amphibious and auxiliary ships have similar proportions of labor inputs and were placed in one group.[4] The mean proportions of various labor inputs in surface combatants, submarines, and underway replenishment ships are significantly different from one another, and so these categories could not be combined. Merchant ships, of which several types were considered, having input proportions different from naval ships but similar to each other, were aggregated, thus establishing the number of functional categories at five: surface combatants, auxiliaries, amphibians, nuclear submarines, and underway replenishment ships. Aircraft carriers were not included in the study. Only one shipyard has the facilities, experience and ability to obtain orders to construct them. Any projected demand for carriers was assigned arbitrarily to that yard.

Further distinctions within these five categories were made in order to take account of differences in yard size and capability. Some yards can produce only part of the ships included in a single category. Thus, it was necessary to break down the categories by size. Length distinctions were made within functional categories to assure that ships would be limited to building positions of appropriate size. Also, ships requiring special capabilities not present in every yard (such as nuclear qualifications) appear as separate shipbuilding activities.

Table 2-2 shows the number of size groupings within each functional category and indicates the number of individual design classes that were consolidated by function. Each of the 10 size groups in the second column appears in the model as a separate shipbuilding activity. The range of ship design classes indicates that the large ship procurement program involves the consideration of ship types not included at all in the smaller program. In the case of amphibious and auxiliary ships in the small program, for instance, four ship classes were combined by size into two shipbuilding activities in the model. Where there was more than one

Table 2-2
The Grouping of Ships for the Model*

Major Functional Categories	No. of Size Groupings (Model "Activities")	No. of Design Classes
Surface Combatants		
Nuclear-powered	1	1
Nonnuclear	1	2
Nuclear submarines	1	1-2
Underway replenishment	2	2
Amphibious and auxiliary	2	4-5
Merchant ships and tankers (including MSTS)	3	5
Total	10	15-17

*Aircraft carriers are not included.

ship class within an activity, weighted average coefficients were calculated for cost and resource use.

3 Factor Supplies, Productivity, and Investment

The potential output and cost structure of a shipyard are determined by its initial endowments of capital and labor and its ability to enhance the productivity of these factors through investment or reorganization. With the exception of one new yard, construction techniques in the United States are fundamentally the same in all yards. Productivity differences that exist result primarily from differences in the age and size of equipment and in the composition of labor force. Thus, a comparative analysis of shipyards must begin with an examination of the equipment and labor supplies at their disposal.

Detailed comparison of the production processes and factor availabilities at each yard yielded information that was used to treat two related problems. The first is that of obtaining the relative financial cost of building each ship in each yard. These costs are in large measure a function of differences in labor usage and wage costs. How this question was handled is discussed in considerable detail in Chapter 3.

The second problem is that of measuring the real resources required for the production activities of each yard in order to convert a yard's capacity as measured by available inputs into capacity as measured by output. Essentially this is equivalent to the problem of obtaining a production function for each yard. An explicit production function was not derived but is nevertheless implicit in the analytical model described in Chapter 5, which utilizes the data described in this chapter.

3-1 Capital Equipment and Labor Productivity

The shipbuilding process can be subdivided into two major phases:

1. Hull construction—the preparation and assembly of large pieces of steel into subsections of a ship and the integration of these subsections on a shipways or platform or in a building dock
2. Outfitting—the installation of engines, equipment, and electrical components

Corresponding to this breakdown of production activities, the skilled labor required to build ships was allocated into three categories. These are the skill groups employed in (1) hull construction, (2) electrical installations, and

(3) mounting of other components. The latter two skill categories are used primarily in the outfitting phase and were combined into one group called *outfitting labor* in analyzing productivity differences.

As a basis for measuring differences in labor productivity, an inventory was taken of equipment in each of the yards. Different mixes and availability of equipment and technique meant that different amounts of labor for hull erection and outfitting were required in each yard. These labor requirements were used to obtain indices of labor productivity.

Hull-erection Productivity

The hull-erection process in a modernized yard is the most capital-intensive of the construction stages. As a result, labor-productivity differences between old and new processes can be significant. Estimates of labor productivity in hull erection were based on the potential decrease in labor time effected through the use of the different types of equipment shown in Table 3-1. Most of the potential labor savings are extremely large, but some of the items affect only a small component of the total shipbuilding process.[1] Table 3-2 in the following section gives a more complete picture of the relationship between crane capacity and the productivity of hull labor.

Outfitting Productivity

It is the consensus of the industry that the greatest potential for saving labor in building ships is in the outfitting portion of the process. Outfitting

Table 3-1
Percent Man-hour Saving from Advanced Equipment Compared to the Least Efficient Method in Use

Shipbuilding Process	Percent Man-hour Saving
Fairing and lofting	
Optically controlled	44
Numerically controlled	89-96
Numerically guided drafting	98
Automatic plate handling	85
Automatic plate cleaning and priming	96
Plate cutting	
Optically guided	80
Numerically guided	90
Assembly–200-ton crane	12

Source: Interviews with equipment makers and shipyard officials.

Table 3-2
Percent Man-hour Savings from Increasing Lifting Capability at the Building Positions

Maximum Lifting Capability (tons)	Savings, Compared with 50-ton Crane: Hull Integration	50-ton Crane: Outfitting	Next Smaller Crane: Hull Integration	Next Smaller Crane: Outfitting
75	2.4	3.8	2.4	3.8
100	4.6	8.3	2.2	4.5
125	7.2	12.3	2.6	4.0
150	9.0	15.5	1.8	3.2
175	10.7	18.0	1.7	2.5
200	12.3	19.5	1.6	1.5

Source: Interviews with shipyard officials.

comprises from 60 to 80 percent of total man-hours required for a complex ship and is a highly labor-intensive activity.

The most important considerations that affect labor requirements and costs of outfitting can be listed under three headings:

1. Crane lift capability at the docks, ways, or integration platform
2. Planning and scheduling of parts and materials and of the production flow
3. The physical characteristics and layout of the yard, such as proximity of storage sheds, pipe-fitting shops, machine shops, and other facilities to the outfitting piers, docks, and platen areas

Items 2 and 3 offer no possibility for quantification and can be compared only in the most general way between yards. As a result, crane lift capability alone was used as a proxy for productivity in outfitting. Assuming there are associated improvements in planning and yard layout, a greater capability to lift preassembled and preoutfitted ship sections will permit much of the outfitting to be done more efficiently away from the ways, dock, or platform, thus increasing labor productivity.

Figure 3-1 shows the relationship suggested by one yard between the lift capability at the ways and the number of lifts needed to construct a small tanker. The yard's estimate of labor savings also is shown. If the combined hoist capability is increased from 80 to 150 tons per lift, larger sections can be handled, and the number of sections to be lifted into place can be reduced by about 80 percent. In this way, approximately 6 percent of the ship's outfitting labor inputs can be saved. If lifting equipment capable of 200-ton hoists is installed, the number of lifts required can be reduced to 58, but the additional labor saving is estimated at only 1 percent. These savings may be more or less, depending on the type of ship being built.

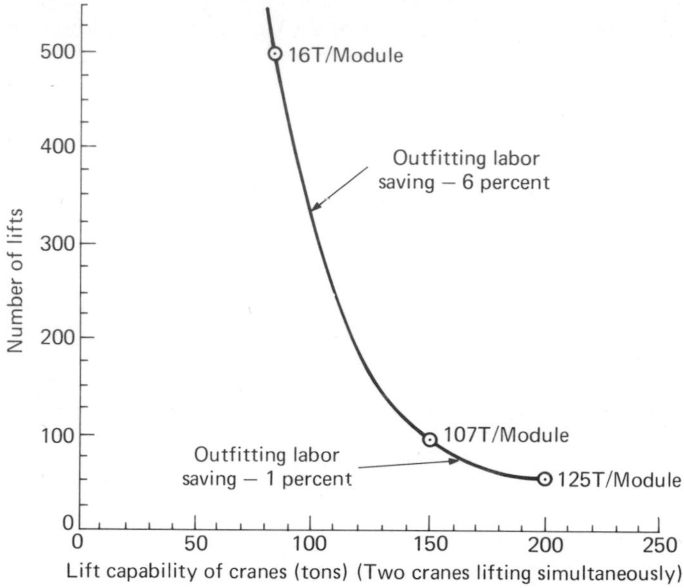

Figure 3–1. The relationship between the number of lifts and crane capability in construction of a small tanker.

Other yards provided considerably larger estimates of potential manpower savings to be obtained from increasing maximum lifting capability at the ways or docks. This could be a result of their envisioning more thoroughgoing preoutfitting and improvements in preoutfitting techniques, compared with those assumed above.

Savings in hull-construction manpower are also possible with larger cranes. Construction of larger modules permits more efficient welding methods. The expected rates of labor savings are shown for both the hull integration and outfitting phases in Table 3-2. They are given as percents of the labor utilized in each of these functions. Both the total saving as compared with the use of a 50-ton crane and the marginal saving due to an incremental increase in crane capacity are listed.

3-2 Ship Labor Inputs and Yard Labor Supplies

The amount of labor required to build a particular ship varies inversely with the relative efficiency of labor use in each yard. The differences among yards in equipment holdings and production techniques provided a basis for estimating the relative productivities. The productivities in turn were used to derive production coefficients relating output in each yard to the amounts of labor resources used. The production coefficients used to arrive at a measure of output capacity are essential parameters for the analytical model discussed in Chapter 5. They are also needed, in conjunction with an estimate of total labor availability, to determine the shape and location of the cost curve, particularly the output level at which costs begin to rise.

Labor Requirements and Productivity

Throughout the study it was assumed that, wherever feasible, ship orders would be let in lots equal to the total demand for a particular type of ship. As a result, the productivity levels and labor production coefficients were calculated for each yard as though it were either producing the total order or had reached the minimum-cost capacity level if smaller than the order.

The labor input parameters for each yard and ship were derived in three steps. First, standard first-ship direct labor requirements were estimated from data on past bids.[2] These labor requirements were broken down into two categories: (1) hull construction and (2) electrical and nonelectrical outfitting. Second, an index of relative labor productivity by yard was calculated for each of the labor categories. The two indices were then used to adjust separately the standard amount of hull labor and the standard amount of outfitting labor required for each ship to obtain first-ship labor requirements in each yard. Since the average amount of labor needed per ship is considerably less for a large production run than the amount required for the first vessel, the third step consisted of adjusting the first-ship labor requirements to take account of the "learning effect" or the efficiencies that are engendered by long production runs. The production coefficients finally obtained were labeled *bid-lot labor requirements* and provided an estimate of how much skilled labor was required per ship under the assumption that the yard was producing either at capacity or, if below capacity, it was nevertheless producing the entire order.

The productivity indices used in the second step were estimated by comparing equipment holdings and techniques in the various yards. The index for hull labor was determined by the amount and quality of the steel processing equipment in each yard, while that for outfitting labor was a function of crane capacity. The indices are shown in Table 3-3 with the base being an arbitrarily chosen yard of intermediate efficiency. The larger the index number, the less efficient the yard. The last column in the table illustrates the relative total amount of skilled labor required for a ship whose labor inputs are 35 percent hull and 65 percent outfitting.

The learning effect of step three was calculated using a 93.2 percent learning curve (see Appendix A). In other words, for each doubling of production level, 6.8 percent less labor is required, on average, to build the ships. The yards were

Table 3-3
Indices of Manpower Use by Yard

Region and Shipyard	Hull Construction	Outfitting and Electronics	Illustrative Ship*
New Yard	52	82	72
Southern			
Yard 1	88	99	95
Yard 2	100	100	100
Yard 3	119	100	107
Eastern†			
Yard 4	85	104	97
Yard 5	92	102	98
Yard 6	96	86	89
Yard 7	97	99	98
Yard 8	120	102	108
Yard 9	144	99	115
Yard 10	147	103	118
Western			
Yard 11	101	102	102
Yard 12	103	105	104
Yard 13	105	96	99
Yard 14	148	105	120

*This column shows an index of labor inputs for a ship for which 35 percent of the labor is for hull construction and 65 percent for outfitting and electronics.

†One shipyard located in the Great Lakes area is included in this group.

permitted to continue down the learning curve until they reached one of two possible constraints, the total size of the order or the initial capacity of the yard as measured by its labor input availability.

The Initial Labor Supply–1967 Base

The implicit production function used in the study required an estimate of the initial endowment of labor resources in each yard in order to establish the location of the cost curve and to provide a production point which could be labeled the minimum cost capacity level. Any such estimate that is based on employment data will be somewhat arbitrary since employment depends upon production at a point in time. The level of demand in the industry has fluctuated sufficiently that the choice of a time period pretty well predetermines the figures one will get for labor endowments. Since there seemed to be no valid reason for favoring one time period over another, the most recent available data, that for 1967, was used.

To arrive at numbers related to production activities, estimates were made of total shipyard employment levels and of the number of workers engaged in conversion and repair. The conversion and repair figures were subtracted from the yard's total labor force to obtain the manpower available for new construction. An assumption was made that no workers would be transferred subsequently from repair to new construction (see Appendix C). Unskilled workers were then subtracted to arrive at the number of skilled workers available for new ship construction at the beginning of the two-year period. The results, aggregated by region, are shown in Table 3-4. They include estimates for the (then not yet operational) Litton yard.

The mix of labor skills in a yard will depend upon the kinds and quantities of ships being built. As the composition of orders changes over time, so will the distribution of workers' skills. Choice of a different date as the base point for employment would have yielded a different skill distribution. Fortunately, the model used to analyze the allocation of ship contracts is rather insensitive to the initial distribution of labor skills. For example, if each yard's total employment is allocated into skill categories so as to reproduce the aggregate industry distribution, the optimal construction pattern is nearly the same as that derived using the actual 1967 labor distributions. This insensitivity results because both the comparative and absolute cost differentials among yards depend primarily upon the yard's endowments of capital equipment and the regional wage differentials, rather than skill distribution.

Expansion and Contraction of the Labor Force

Yards incur increased marginal costs when they build ships at a rate requiring any type of labor in excess of the initial work force. The addition of workers to expand production imposes costs at the outset because the new work force is likely to be less efficient and may require some training. There may also be costs

Table 3-4
Initial Skilled Employment for New Construction by Region and Category*

Region	Hull Erection	Outfitting	Electrical	Totals	Percent
Southern	5,100	6,200	1,400	12,700	36
Eastern†	6,900	8,000	2,600	17,500	50
Western	2,500	1,700	500	4,700	14
Totals					
Employees	14,500	15,900	4,500	34,900	
Percentages	42	46	12		100

*Based on 1967 data.

†One Great Lakes yard included.

involved in reorganizing production activities. The majority of these costs are likely to be encountered only once, however, for a given expansion of employment. Once new workers are integrated into the permanent labor force, the cost of using them is no different from that for the original workers.

Theoretically it is costless to reduce the labor force by laying off personnel. A yard might be reluctant to lay off all the redundant people it may have at some point in time, however, if it expects that it may need them back in the near future. The expected cost of maintaining a larger-than-necessary labor force over some period may be less than the expected cost of increasing the labor pool at some future date.

3-3 Ways and Docks as the Output Constraint

Given an initial endowment of labor and an unconstrained labor market so that a shipyard can hire as many new workers as it may wish, provided it is willing to pay for them, the upper limit on capacity is a capital constraint. Although investment in some forms of capital equipment is presumed to be feasible for the yards, the study assumes that the physical size of the yards and the number of ship construction positions in each is fixed at the number currently in existence. This does not preclude the possibility of constructing new yards, but such potential construction is analyzed separately.

For any particular yard, the limit on the rate of production is determined by the number of existing ways and docks. The maximum production rate differs according to the size and complexity of the ship being built. The upper limit for any ship can be increased by investing in capital equipment, particularly large cranes which permit larger modules to be constructed outside the ways position and thus reduce the time required from keel-laying to launch. The potential saving on construction time is small, however, without a total renovation of yard organization and production patterns.

Number of Usable Building Positions

The 14 old shipyards under study had over 60 active shipways and building docks between 460 and 960 feet long. Details on these were provided by the yards themselves. The new Litton facility at Pascagoula has a single launching position for elevator launching of ships of 1,000 feet or more in length.

All building positions were classified into three categories by length. A single yard might have ways in each category. The number of active ways and docks in each region is shown by size in Table 3-5. Over half of the building positions, including almost all those adequate for very large ships, are located in the East.

Table 3-5
Ways and Docks Capacity by Region

Region	Small (460 to 600 ft)	Medium (620 to 725 ft)	Large (over 725 ft)	Total
Gulf Coast	13	6	1	20
East Coast*	15	10	10	35
West Coast	7	2	0	9
Total	35	18	11	64

*One Great Lakes yard included.

3-4 Capital Investments

The Theory of Investment

Some capital equipment in many shipyards has existed since World War II. This is particularly true of most ways and building docks and of the physical yard layout. There is little doubt that productivity could be increased through modernization in most yards. A decision to invest, however, is a function of expectations concerning the probability of receiving a government contract in the future. Widely fluctuating demands and uncertainty in the number and value of future additions to the naval and merchant fleets inhibit investment. These conditions also make it difficult to predict future investment expenditures. For purposes of analysis, however, we assumed that if production were forecast to be undertaken in any yard, then new investment would also take place if it would pay for itself through savings in labor cost.

There are two fundamental kinds of investment. One is replacement of obsolete equipment and modernization of facilities. The other is construction of entirely new facilities. The two alternatives are analyzed separately in this study. Initially we shall consider the modernization aspect, leaving discussion of new yards or expansion of old ones until later.

Investment in more efficient equipment and methods affects two elements of the shipbuilding process: costs and capacity. The greater the amount of investment, the lower the marginal and average costs of production will be. In addition, investment typically increases construction capacity directly, by increasing the amount of equipment, and indirectly, by replacing inefficient machines with those that either require less labor or produce more output per unit of time or both. Figure 3-2 shows in three dimensions the effects of investment on the usual two-dimensional cost curve under the assumption that the investment is infinitely devisible and the cost function is continuously differentiable at all points. Investment reduces both marginal and average costs, but at a decreasing rate. It also increases capacity. The line AB traces out in

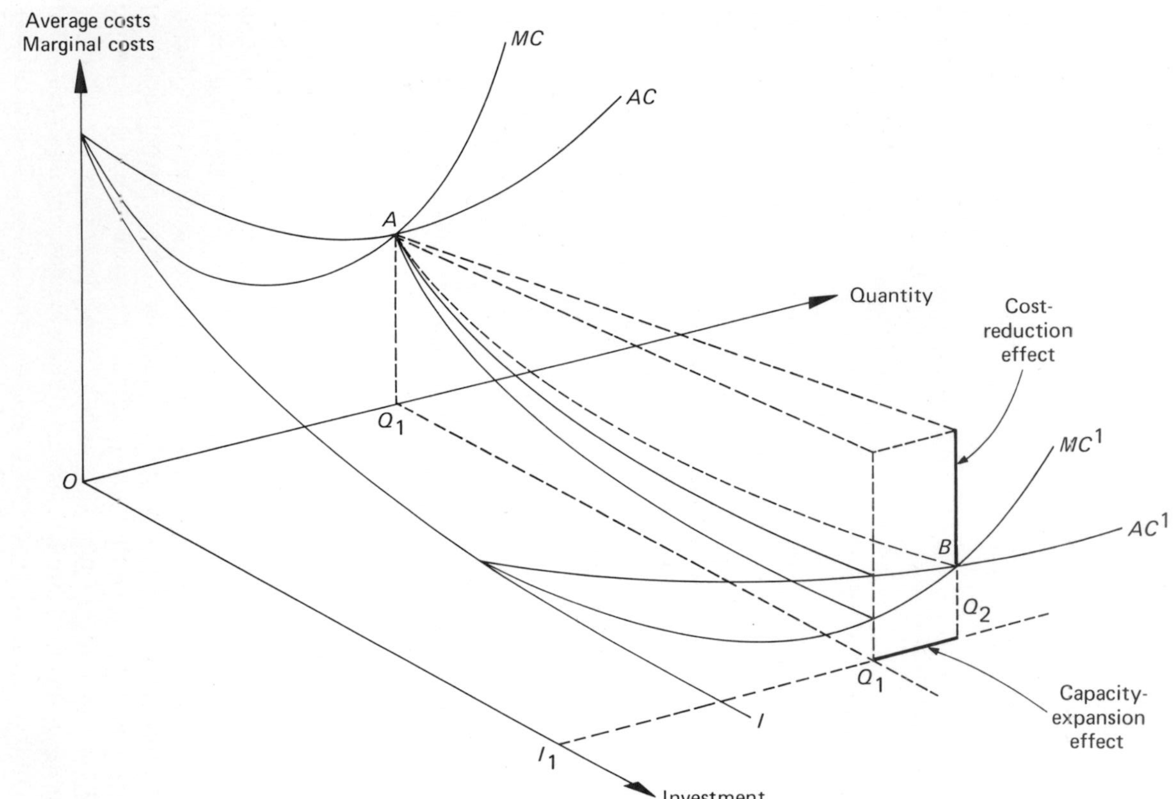

Figure 3–2. The effects of investment on costs and capacity.

three dimensions the path of the point at which marginal costs equal average costs for any amount of new investment. This is the point at which a yard would construct ships under conditions of competitive equilibrium.

As we have discussed earlier, however, the usual two-dimensional cost curves are totally inadequate to describe a multi-product, multi-input firm. The concepts are equally unsatisfactory for outlining the effects of investment on costs and capacity. In the first place, investment is invariably discrete. As a result, there is no smooth change in the marginal costs or capacity, but rather, an abrupt drop in the former and a rise in the latter as a lump of investment is undertaken. In the second place, it is quite possible that investment will reduce the cost of production and increase labor productivity in one area of a facility without affecting costs in another part. For example, the installation of a new, heavy-lift crane on one of several ways might make it cheaper to build ships on that way without affecting costs on the others. The marginal cost of constructing ships with the new crane would decline, while that of the remainder would remain unchanged. Increased investment would thus provide some capacity to produce at the new lower cost rather than lead to lower costs for all ships produced. Cost reduction will also be a function of the kinds of ships produced since not all ship types will be affected in the same way by a decision to invest in some particular piece of equipment.

Individual Yards

The multidimensionality of the effects of investment are taken into account in the analysis. As will be explained more fully in Chapter 4, the description of the firm in terms of a two-dimensional cost curve was discarded in favor of a more realistic and revealing model which defines the firm as a set of output activities and input constraints. The effects of investment on this set of characteristics within each yard can be fully taken into account.

The total potential investment in improved equipment and the effects it has on costs and labor productivity is different for each shipyard. Investment in the new yard is likely to have little effect on costs, because it presumably already has the most modern available equipment and construction methods. The investment possibilities and their effects for the other yards will depend upon the amount of modern equipment they already have and the kind of construction process they use. Estimating this potential required that the technological characteristics of each yard be examined individually, in order to determine the kinds and quantities of new equipment that could be introduced would engender. There was no way in which individual equipment purchases could be predicted or integrated into the analysis. It was possible, however, to generate, from the examination of equipment needs of individual yards, a composite investment function for each yard that lumps potential equipment purchases into *investment units*. A unit, which is measured only in terms of a dollar value, is $100,000 worth of investment.

In each yard, purchase of one unit of investment results in a reduction of the cost of building ships and an increase in the capacity to build at the lower price. It also results in a reduction of the amount of labor required per ship and in the amount of time the ship must remain on the ways, or in the dock. Thus, total capacity of the yard is effectively increased. The proportion by which cost falls and capacity rises for a certain ship category depends upon the importance of the improved phase of the shipbuilding process in that ship's construction. The values of these cost, time, and labor savings by skill category were estimated for each yard individually by examining its current mix of equipment and by projecting potential acquisitions and the changes in construction methods that would result.

Not all new equipment yields the same return or increased labor productivity, however. Each piece is different, and it was possible to rank the potential investments in roughly descending order of desirability for each yard. After ranking, equipment was placed into two categories, one of which had higher returns and greater productivity increases than the other. The value of potential investment in the higher return category defined the number of $100,000 investment units that could be permitted at that return. The remainder of the total potential investment for each yard would yield a lower return. Once a yard is completely modernized, no further investment is of value.[3]

The question of investment in totally new facilities, either by yards currently operating or by potential competitors, was examined in a quite different manner from that of investment for modernization. The initial analysis assumed that modernization would take place, whenever profitable, concurrently with production. It did not consider, however, the possibility of constructing completely new capacity. Evaluation of whether new capacity would be profitable was done after analyzing how a given level of demand would be distributed among available yards. A comparison was made between the estimated capital value of a new, highly efficient yard and the cost of building such a yard. This was nothing more than a variant of the theoretical technique of comparing the marginal efficiency of capital to the cost of capital.

4 The Estimation of Shipyard Cost Functions

A central concern of this book is the cost and pricing of specified fleets of ships. In this chapter, we discuss the shape and significance of cost functions and examine their role in determining firms' prices and profits. Then we describe the modification of the cost relationships required for the analytic model and the method of estimating numerical parameters.

4-1 The Meaning of Cost Curves and Their Adaptation to the Model

The idealized short-run cost curves for a firm relate cost per unit output to the rate of production and are assumed to behave as illustrated in Figure 4-1. Typically, the average variable cost curve declines until it reaches the rate of production which utilizes the optimal labor complement for existing equipment. This rate of production is generally determined by the single-shift capacity of the shipyard. Beyond this point, marginal and average variable costs rise, as it becomes necessary to utilize overtime and extra shifts with higher wages and lower labor productivity, to hire and train new workers, and perhaps to utilize less efficient machinery or processes.

Competitive bidding by a small number of firms to produce items made to order creates a pricing environment more like competition than oligopoly, but conceptually different from both. Under *perfect competition*, firms become price takers and adjust their outputs to a market-determined price. Economic theory postulates that the equilibrium price gravitates toward the minimum average total cost of the least efficient firm needed to satisfy the demand. Firms having lower cost curves will maximize profits by producing the amount at which marginal cost equals the market price.

With competitive bidding, certain firms, anticipating uncommitted capacity for the period in question and qualified to fulfill the order, submit bids based on their costs and knowledge of competitors' activities. The marginal cost curve (or average variable cost curve, if higher) sets an effective floor for potential bids.[1] How far above marginal cost a firm is willing to bid depends upon its assessment of the competition. The low-cost firms will operate at higher production rates than their less efficient or less well-situated rivals and will tend to produce at the rate where their marginal cost approaches the minimum average total cost of the highest-cost firm. Although there are technical reasons for deviations of winning

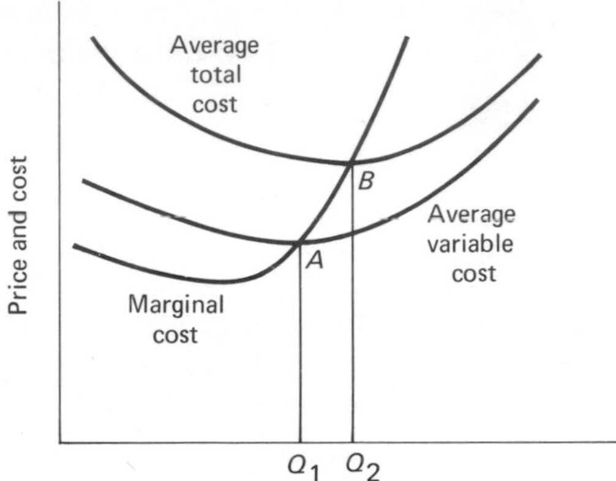

Figure 4–1. Typical cost curves for a firm.

bids from purely competitive price level, the difference would not be great if there were several qualified bidders with no collusion among them.

In a multi-product firm whose output is as complex and differentiated as that of a shipyard, the simple, smooth cost curves of Figure 4-1 are an inadequate representation of reality unless one were able to standardize output in terms of some measure like steel tonnage. Given the differences in sophistication and equipment of various ship types, such a standardization is impossible to achieve and would have little value for the kind of analysis undertaken in this study even if it were feasible.

A much more easily managed representation of costs results if a few assumptions are adopted which make the cost function more closely approach reality in some aspects while distorting it slightly in others. The distortion that is deliberately introduced is the assumption that the total cost function is a piecewise linear function so that the marginal cost curve becomes a step function. Figures 4-2*a* and 4-2*b* show these relationships. The second assumption, which increases the validity of the cost function, is one that cannot be depicted graphically. This is that the cost function is multi-dimensional, with the initial marginal and average variable cost level being a weighted average that is determined by the mix of products actually produced, while the rising portion of the curve is defined by the costs of acquiring factors of production.

These two assumptions permit costs to reflect jointly the type and quantity of output as well as the amount of inputs required. In addition, the problem of comparing costs can be structured in such a way that the productivity and initial availability of labor skills for each shipyard is taken into account.

An additional constraint on the function used to represent costs is imposed by the analytical model chosen (see Chapter 5). The model cannot accomodate

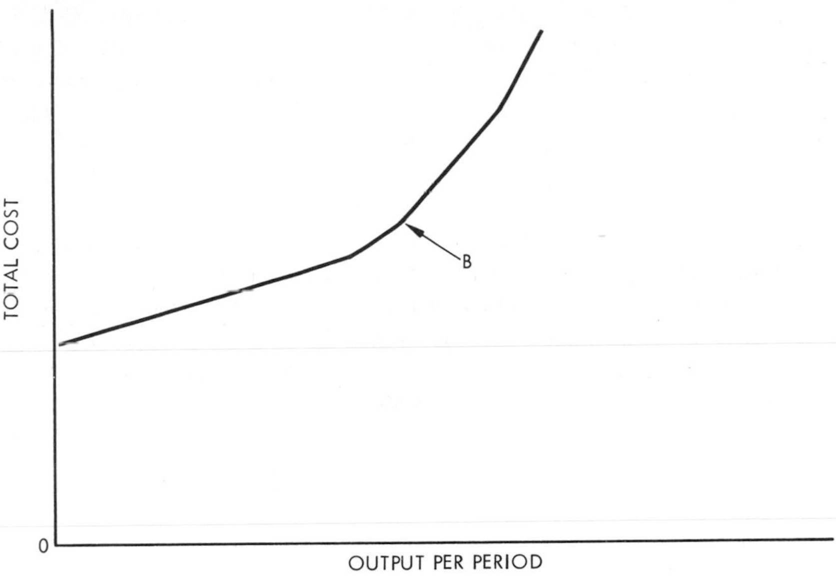

Figure 4–2*a*. Piecewise linear total-cost curve.

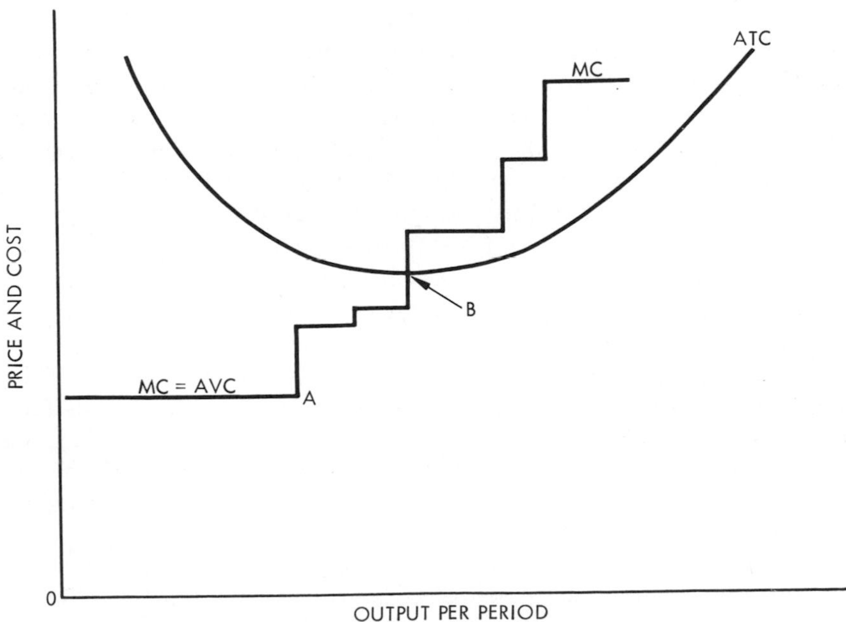

Figure 4–2*b*. Firm cost curve as adapted for the model.

declining costs. Therefore, a single horizontal line is used to approximate the initial portion of the average variable cost curve with the height of this line set equal to the minimum cost point. The minimum cost is estimated separately for each ship program in each qualified yard, as if no other ship type were produced in that yard. This level is chosen *under the assumption that a government contracting policy will be followed which permits single orders to be given for the total quantity of each ship type required.* Thus, yards making successful bids will produce either the entire order for the ship in question or at least as much as they can produce using only their initial labor force.

The upward-sloping portion of the marginal cost curve is approximated by a step function. Each upward step in cost signals that one of a succession of resource constraints has been met as production expands. Each increase represents the cost of increasing the availability of a resource.

4-2 Derivation of Relative Costs

Given the capital equipment in place in the industry, the variable cost of building a particular ship in a particular yard depends upon (1) the size and complexity of the ship, (2) the labor productivity of the yard, (3) the wage rates the yard must pay, and (4) the number of ships in the production run. In making estimates of production costs, all four of these elements were taken into account. For the kind of analysis undertaken in the study, the absolute cost levels were considerably less important than the relative costs between the yards. The major effort in estimating the costs was devoted to comparing wage and productivity levels. Once the relationships were established, one yard was chosen as a standard cost yard and the other yards' costs normalized with respect to that yard so that cost differentials could be expressed in index form.

Since each shipbuilding activity encompasses a conglomerate of ship types, it was necessary to obtain a standard cost for the activity that reflected the kinds and numbers of ships comprising it. Precontract estimates of ship costs involve great uncertainty and, especially for new designs, are extremely tenuous. Even for a specific number of ships of a familiar design, factors like changes in shipyard efficiency and unforeseen design changes during production make cost forecasts hazardous. Since it was not possible to obtain cost estimates for a selection of ships built on specific production facilities, the individual ship costs used in making up the standard cost for an activity were based on the generalized 1968 planning estimates of the U.S. Department of Defense and the Maritime Administration.

Total cost was estimated on a first-of-a-series basis, and this figure was divided between labor, materials, and "overhead" costs. Since only variable costs are important for production decisions, the last was subtracted from the total. The cost assigned to a shipbuilding activity was an average of the costs of the ships included in that category weighted by the numbers of each type to be built. The labor portions of these weighted average costs for each category were made specific for a shipyard by multiplying the standard cost for each ship by the indices of yard productivity and wage rates. The costs thus obtained are henceforth referred to as *first-ship labor costs.*

Calculation of First-ship Costs in Each Yard

Costs were differentiated among yards on the basis of two characteristics: (1) the regional shipyard wage level and (2) the yard's relative efficiency in manpower utilization. Indices for these two characteristics were calculated independently and were then used to adjust the standard first-ship labor costs to make them specific to each yard.

The regional wage differentials in the yards were obtained from U.S. Department of Commerce data. These differentials are shown in Table 4-1 with the index for the East Coast set at 100.[2] Regional differences in the delivered costs of steel and other material inputs were found by the Maritime Administration to be negligible.[3] Thus, for example, if labor cost is 40 percent of shipyard variable cost, then the wage difference would make this ship cost 4 percent lower in the South than on the East Coast and about 5.6 percent higher in the West.

The second step in calculating ship costs for each yard was somewhat more complicated in that it required examining separately the two labor categories, hull and outfitting. The productivity of each category is a function of the amount and kind of capital equipment a yard has at its disposal. An inventory of equipment was made in each yard, and two productivity indices were calculated, one for hull labor and one for outfitting labor. These indices provided a measure of the relative efficiency of the labor in each yard. (See Table 3-3 and Chapter 3-2.) Each ship classification is built, however, with different proportions of hull and outfitting labor. The overall productivity index for a yard thus depends upon the kind of ship under consideration. The productivity index number for a

Table 4-1
Indices of U.S. Shipyard Wages by Region

Region	Index
West Coast	114
East Coast	100
Gulf Coast	90
Great Lakes	87

Source: U.S. Department of Commerce, Maritime Administration, *Relative Costs of Shipbuilding in the Various Coastal Districts of the United States* (Washington, D.C., 1967), pp. 12-13.

particular ship type was obtained by weighting the yard's hull and outfitting productivity indices by the relative amounts of the two categories of labor required in that ship's construction. The weighted productivity index was used in the same manner as the regional wage index to adjust further the standard first-ship labor cost for each ship and to make it specific to the yard. Using a weighted average of the productivities to modify the cost means that yards with efficient steel-processing facilities have a competitive advantage in steelwork intensive ships like general-purpose assault ships (LHAs) and tankers, while those with the largest cranes are able to pre-outfit larger ship sections and therefore have relatively lower costs in building ships with a high proportion of outfitting work.

Once the standardized labor cost for each ship was adjusted by the yard's productivity and regional wage difference, it was then added to the materials cost to arrive at the total variable cost.[4] In this way the cost of building each ship type in each shipyard was obtained.

It is interesting to compare the cost differentials that derive from productivity alone with those that also include the effects of regional wage differences. Figure 4-3 shows the relative costs that are ground out solely by labor productivity differences. The new yard has an impressive advantage in expected labor productivity resulting in 7 to 9 percent lower variable costs for all ships compared with the next most efficient yard. The range of cost differences among all yards varies from 1 to about 20 percent and is smallest for the large and/or highly complex ship types, which only a few yards can build. The figure shows the number of competitors involved, which ranges from 3 for complex nuclear combatants and very large ships to 14 for small merchant ships.

When the regional wage differences are taken into account, the range of costs in different yards increases for most ship types. The maximum range goes up to 30 percent. Table 4-2 shows indices of the regionally adjusted first-ship variable cost. Some ships are omitted in order to conceal the identities of individual yards. Although it is not shown in the table, the wage difference between the Gulf Coast and the East Coast is sufficient to offset the productivity advantages of all but one East Coast yard. West Coast yards as a group have the highest costs inasmuch as they pay the highest wage levels and also have the lowest productivity. The importance of the wage differences in determining relative costs helps explain why the new yard and most yard modernization is in the South. There are no cases in which a yard located in a higher wage area fully compensates by having more efficient facilities.

Some implications of these cost figures should be clarified. Although the yards with higher variable costs will be the last to go into production and last to add new capacity, it does not necessarily follow that these yards, once producing, must make lower profits. A yard with high variable costs because of low labor productivity is probably using a production method involving less capital equipment. As a result, the fixed costs of this firm may be lower. It is

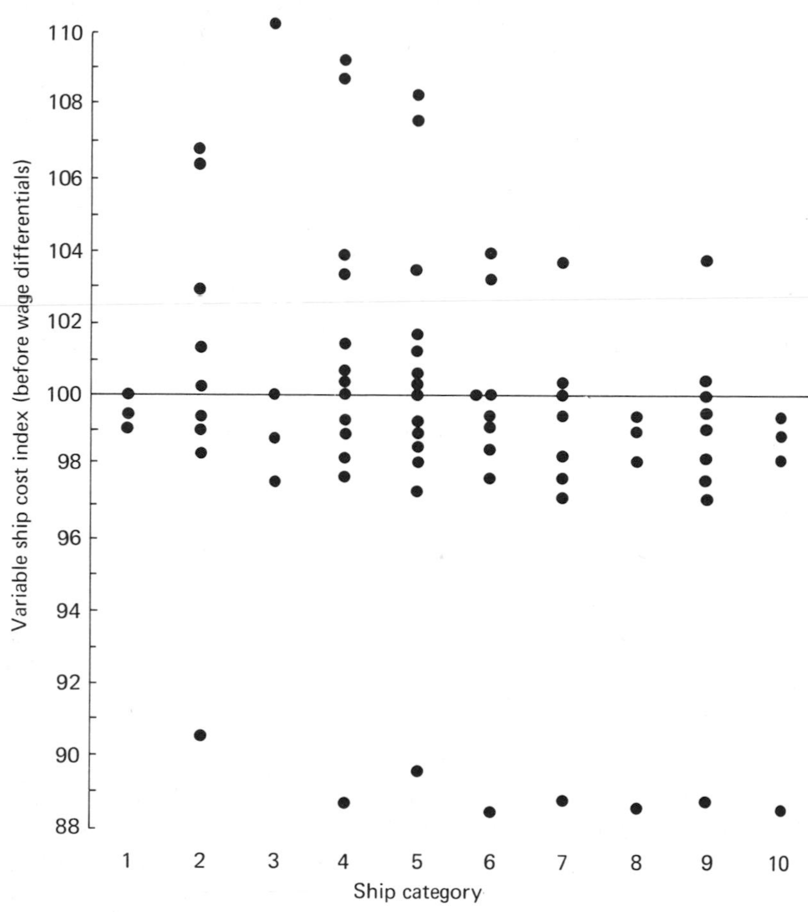

Key to ship categories:

Ship 1	Nuclear combatants	Ship 7	Merchant ships, 600 to 725 ft.
Ship 2	Nonnuclear combatants	Ship 8	Underway replenishment ships (naval) over 725 ft.
Ship 3	Submarines	Ship 9	Tankers, 600 to 725 ft.
Ship 4	Underway replenishment ships (naval) under 600 ft.	Ship 10	Amphibious and auxiliary ships over 725 ft.
Ship 5	Merchant ships under 600 ft.		
Ship 6	Amphibious and auxiliary ships, 600 to 725 ft.		

Figure 4–3. Indices of variable-cost differences among yards due to efficiency of labor and materials use.

Table 4-2
Indices of Fully Differentiated First-Ship Variable Cost in Yards by Region

Shipyard (Rank Order)	Nonnuclear Combatants	Small Replenishment	Small Merchant	Large Noncombatant
New yard	91.2	89.4	90.4	89.0
Gulf Coast yards				
Yard 1	98.5	98.0	98.2	–
Yard 2	100.0	100.0	100.0	100.0
Yard 3	–	103.1	102.7	–
East Coast yards*				
Yard 1	102.4	101.7	101.7	102.2
Yard 2	–	102.5	102.5	103.0
Yard 3	102.7	101.7	102.7	103.1
Yard 4	–	–	100.3	–
Yard 5	106.3	107.6	106.9	–
Yard 6	104.7	106.8	105.9	–
West Coast yards				
Yard 1	108.8	109.4	108.8	–
Yard 2	–	108.9	108.8	–
Yard 3	109.7	110.4	109.7	–
Yard 4	116.0	119.5	117.6	–

*One shipyard located in the midwest is grouped with the East Coast yards to obscure its identity.

conceivable that in a period of high demand for the industry an old yard may earn a greater rate of return at a modest rate of production than a highly capitalized yard with a high rate of activity.

On the other hand, a yard may have high variable costs because it is located in a high-wage area. In this case, given equally capital-intensive methods and equal labor productivity, the higher cost yard indeed will receive a lower return on its capital than yards in regions with lower wages. This could help to explain the concentration of new investment in the industry in the South today.

Derivation of Cost Curves from First-ship Costs

The first-ship costs described in the preceding section are only single points on the average variable cost curves, the points nearest the vertical axis. The remainder of the downward-sloping part of the curves in each yard were estimated using a cost progress function, or *learning curve.* A learning curve is a logarithmic relationship between the average variable cost and the number of units of output. For example, a 93 percent learning curve is generated if costs fall 7 percent each time output is doubled. From an analytical point of view, the most important point on the cost curve is the average variable cost of building the number of ships for which an order is received, since it is this cost, and not the first-ship cost, that would be one of the determinants of the firm's bidding activities.

This bid-lot cost corresponds in most cases to the minimum point on the average variable cost curve, simply because the firm cannot expand output of a single ship type beyond the amount of total demand. Thus there are no further learning economies that can be achieved beyond that point. It is possible, however, that a yard may come up against one or more initial labor-resource constraints before it can produce the total order. In this case, the production level at which the constraint is reached becomes the low point of the average variable cost curve and is determinant of the bid-lot cost. Costs rise from that point on since new labor must be hired or trained.

The bid-lot cost is calculated separately for labor and materials, since the progress coefficient for labor is estimated to be 93.2 percent (taking account of non-recurring set-up costs) while that for materials is 98 percent. The sum of the average labor and materials costs for the bid lot is used as the minimum point on the average variable cost curve of Figure 4-1 and corresponds to the horizontal portion of the linear step function of Figure 4-2*b*.

Since each ship type has a different cost in each yard, there is no unique cost curve for the yard. The location of the horizontal part of the cost curve depicted in Figure 4-2*b* will be an average of the bid-lot costs of the ships being produced. If the total volume of orders requires more labor than the yard initially possesses, the additional resources can be obtained at higher cost. A yard may expand any of its three labor-force components by 30 percent at a 20 percent increase in labor cost. It can expand an additional 30 percent at a 38 percent increase in cost. Additional expansion of labor, up to the yards' ways capacity, incurs a 64 percent higher cost.[5] These higher variable costs correspond to the rising part of the step function of Figure 4-2*b*.

Materials costs are assumed to remain constant over any range of production since shipyards are not dominant users of commodities like steel, pipe, and paint. As a result, the marginal cost of a ship rises by a smaller percentage than do the labor costs alone as the labor-capacity bounds are exceeded. If labor costs were one-third of the variable costs, for example, the cost increases for each ship would be one-third of the percentages given in the previous paragraph.

Some of the costs of expanding the labor force, such as recruitment and training costs and inefficiency due to inexperience, are one-time costs that do not recur. Others, such as night-shift pay differentials, continue. For simplicity, we make the assumption that the increased labor cost continues for one four-year period, but that the labor force on hand at the end of the four years becomes the new capacity level from which expansion and its associated costs are to be measured.

4-3 Discounting of Future Costs

The total present cost of having a fleet available at some future date depends not only on the efficiency of the yards in which the ships are built but also on the time distribution of construction. The later the ships are built, the lower the present value of their cost, assuming that there is an alternative use for the funds and assuming that real factor payments do not rise. To take account of the opportunity cost of capital and to make comparable the costs of different ship procurement schedules, the future building costs were discounted at an annual interest rate of 10 percent. This rate is an estimate of the after-tax rate of return to private capital.

Discounting of costs provides incentive to the purchaser to postpone construction unless the ships are required early in the decade. If the interest were high and the timing of ship acquisition were not constrained, then no ships would be produced in the first period, while all shipyards–including the least efficient–would be working at capacity in the final period. If the interest rate were sufficiently low, however, it would not pay to postpone construction if it meant facing a peak in activity in a later period which required utilization of inefficient yards.

4-4 Changes in Real Costs of Ships over Time

Changes in real factor costs not offset by productivity increases may raise future real costs of ships relative to values of other commodities. It should be emphasized, however, that changes in ship costs at the same pace as those in other prices in the economy (general inflation) would not affect ship procurement decisions. Only the *difference* between cost increases for ships and those of alternative purchases is significant.

If ship costs change at a rate different from the general price level, but by the same proportion in all yards, the optimal timing of ship construction could be affected, but not the relative construction costs of the yards. The effect of a uniform change in real ship costs on the optimal procurement schedule could be taken into account by lowering the discount rate by the amount by which ship-cost inflation exceeds general inflation, or by raising the rate if ship costs lag behind. If shipyard costs change differently among regions or if relative factor prices change, more complicated adjustments would be required.

5 A Linear Programming Model of the U.S. Shipbuilding Industry

Thus far the study has examined the shipbuilding industry in terms of its structural and behavioral characteristics, attempting to highlight the important attributes of the demand function and to define and measure the parameters that distinguish the production functions identified with each yard. In order to evaluate the effects of different demand levels and make meaningful comparisons among yards, it was necessary to fit the structural observations into an analytical model capable of answering the major questions posed by the study.

There are a number of techniques that could have been used to examine the overall performance of the shipbuilding industry and make policy comparisons, but a linear programming model seemed to possess the most useful set of characteristics. It is a method that involves optimization of a linear objective function subject to a set of linear constraints.[1] The linearity assumptions are the primary limiting factor in using programming as an analytical tool, but this limitation is outweighed by the advantages the technique offers. Such a model permits the simultaneous examination of shipbuilding activities in all the yards included in the study and makes feasible multilateral comparisons of costs and resource requirements that would be quite impossible with any other analytical method, given the size and nature of the problem.

The main activities included in the objective function are those of building ships in each yard. The constraints which help determine the level at which each activity operates are of two types. The first are those which have resulted from decisions made by individual firms over a period of time in response to market forces. They define the production function and delineate the capacity and special capabilities of each yard. They are in part functions of the industry structure. The second are those that are policy- or demand-determined. They are the result of government decisions about the size of total demand, the timing of orders, changes in the lot size in which orders are made, and attempts to spread work.

To illustrate how the first kinds of constraints affect ship allocations, suppose that one yard has superior lofting and cutting equipment that saves labor mainly in the hull-erection phase of ship construction. Another yard has equipment and techniques that save man-hours in outfitting. Then, if both yards participate in ship construction, the former would tend to specialize in ships for which a high proportion of the variable cost is in steelwork and hull erection, e.g., big, uncomplicated ships like fast-deployment logistics ships (FDLs) and tankers. The latter yard would specialize in ships requiring intensive outfitting. Furthermore, since we distinguish different regional wage levels, but find no significant distinctions in materials costs, then yards in the South with low labor costs would tend to receive orders for labor-intensive ships.

The model assigns contracts for new ships as though all orders for a four-year period were awarded simultaneously in response to bids from each yard. The bid prices are the marginal cost (or average variable cost, if higher) for each ship under the assumption that the yard has no backlog of work for the period in question.

If bids and awards were made in this way and the data were accurate, then the optimal solution would presumably closely replicate the actual future production activities of the various yards for a specified collection of ships. Neither precondition, however, is adequately met for the results to be valid in such detail. In reality, ship orders are awarded sequentially rather than simultaneously with long periods between bidding sessions. Therefore, the actual distribution of production among yards would typically be somewhat different from that indicated by the model. Also, actual bids are always conditioned by the volume of orders already scheduled in the yard, which in turn depends on the sequence in which programs are offered for bid.

Despite these departures from reality, the model is highly informative because the mix of yards receiving contracts and the volume of work in each specific yard should strongly resemble the real world. Moreover, the distribution of production that minimizes the resource costs of ship construction also should minimize the bill to the government. This bill can be estimated using the "shadow prices" of ships (see Section 5-5).[2]

5-1 The Objective Cost Function

The objective function to be minimized is a cost function. It encompasses all variable costs of shipbuilding, including materials costs, the cost of the initial labor force, the cost of acquiring and utilizing additional labor with unaltered capital facilities, the cost of investment in new equipment, and the savings in labor from this investment. It also includes a small component representing the opportunity cost of building small ships on large building positions.

The definitions of the cost coefficients used and the way in which they were estimated are discussed in Chapter 3. In the objective function, each of these coefficients is assigned to the proper shipbuilding activity in each yard. The construction costs in all possible locations for building ships within a particular time period are examined before the ships are allocated to the least-cost yards. As part of the process of comparing costs, the model takes account of the increasing costs that yards incur if they expand production beyond the capacity provided by the initial labor force without increasing the amount of capital. Each yard can increase the number of ships it produces by hiring more labor and paying the price of doing so. As discussed earlier, the labor expansion costs include not only the effects of an upward-sloping labor-supply curve, but also the other costs of expanding output in the short run, such as overtime differentials and less efficient combinations of men and machines.

The costs of investing in more modern equipment are also included in the objective function. Investment in such things as improved drafting methods, steel processing, and larger cranes yields production savings in terms of real resources as well as dollars. Only the dollar savings, however, are reflected in the function. The resource savings are taken into account by adjusting the production coefficients. The total cost function generated is piecewise linear, rather than a smooth curve.

5-2 Ship Demand and Scheduling

The demand for each ship category is inserted into the linear program in the form of a constraint which requires that a certain number of ships be built in each time period but permits any qualified yard to construct them. Two different levels of total demand were considered. The smaller presumed an annual average production of 36 ships, while the larger averaged 69 ships per year. The demand constraints were the instruments through which the effects of scheduling alternatives were evaluated. Different delivery schedules were tested by adjusting demand requirements in different periods without changing total demand.

5-3 Constraints on Resource Use

Labor Use

Skilled labor in each yard is placed into three mutually exclusive categories: outfitting, electrical, and hull-erection labor. Each yard has an initial pool of each type of labor and faces an upward-sloping labor-supply curve should it attempt to hire more. The amount of labor used per ship depends on the type of ship, the yard's equipment, and the length of the yard's production run for that ship. The greater the production run, the more efficient the process becomes and the fewer the number of man-hours required. If a yard's output is expanded beyond the point at which any type of labor is fully utilized, it becomes necessary to employ more people and incur higher production costs. It is assumed that yards in which some labor remains unused in any period, will lay off and lose half of the unused manpower before the next period.

Shipways Time Constraint

The number of shipways and building docks in each yard is held constant in the model. In none of our examples are the industry's existing ways fully utilized in any one period. Major expansion of ways and docks facilities in the industry involves not merely an increase in yard capacity of the type existing in most yards but a reorganization of the entire production process to incorporate modernized techniques. Because changes of this nature in every yard are difficult to encompass in the model, we permitted the number of ways to vary only in the experiment described in Chapter 10, from which we forecast the construction of new yard capacity.

The ways are classified according to size, and a separate constraint applies to each size category. Building each ship requires a certain amount of time on a shipway of some minimum size. Smaller ships can be built on ways larger than this minimum, although the unnecessary use of this option is deterred by assessing a small cost. Large ships, of course, cannot be built on smaller ways.

The policy options concerned with maintaining a mobilization base in the shipbuilding industry were examined by manipulating the ways constraints (see Chapter 9). Maintaining productive facilities involves keeping both capital and labor active. The levels to be maintained in the study, however, were stated in terms of ways capacity under the assumption that sufficient labor would automatically be retained if the ways were being used.

5-4 Investments and Cost Reduction

Each yard is limited in the kind and quantity of capital investment it can undertake to reduce its labor and ways time per ship. The limits are set by the amount of modern steel processing equipment, lofting capability, and crane capacity that each already possesses. Modern yards have little or no opportunity or need to improve their production since their present equipment is already of the newest type. These limits are also determined by yard size and the kinds of ships it builds. (See Appendix H for details on these limits.)

5-5 "Shadow Prices"

One of the most useful aspects of the linear programming model is that it provides "shadow prices" for each of the constraints under which the system operates. The shadow price can be defined as the marginal change in total cost that results from changing the constraint level by one unit. It is therefore the marginal value of having an additional unit of input available or the marginal cost of an additional unit of output. The two most interesting sets of shadow prices are those on demand for ships and the ways capacity.

The shadow price on each demand constraint provides the industry marginal cost of an additional ship during that period (see Appendix B). If competitive behavior prevails, this cost would approximate the winning-bid price for the contract. Shadow prices increase with the total number of ships demanded, since less and less efficient resources must be brought into use. These prices can be used to estimate the budget cost to the government of any shipbuilding program. A summation of the products of the shadow prices and the number of ships for each type would yield the approximate budget cost of procuring the ships.

In contrast, the optimal value of the objective function is the minimum variable production *cost* to the firms. It includes heterogeneous items such as the cost of building ships at the optimal output rate, that of expanding employment with associated diseconomies, and so on. As noted earlier, the difference between summed prices and summed variable production costs is the revenue available to cover fixed costs and profit.

The shadow price of the ways constraint on each yard can be interpreted as the amount a yard should be willing to pay in order to rent another ways, complete with all necessary equipment, for one year. This imputed rental value could be compared with the actual capital cost of a similar facility in order to determine the implicit rate of return on capital in each of the yards.[3] The ways shadow price of the most efficient yard is particularly interesting because it measures the value not only of expanding that yard but also of completely modifying the production function. It also reflects the difference in cost between building ships in the most efficient yard and building them in the next most efficient yard that *still has some capacity available*. Clearly, which yard fulfills the latter definition depends upon total demand, and as demand increases, this efficiency difference also increases.

Part III
Simulation Results

Introduction to Part III

The linear programming model discussed in the last chapter is as close an approximation to the actual structure of the shipbuilding industry as it was possible to construct and still retain a computationally feasible analytical apparatus. The assumptions upon which it is based appear reasonable; the parameters used were, for the most part, empirical estimates, although some were evaluations made by people in the industry; the aggregation of variables, where necessary, was done so as to preserve the essential characteristics of each.

Nevertheless, as with any workable model of a complex structure some modification of reality was necessary. These modifications were discussed in Part II and should be kept in mind in drawing any conclusions from the results of the simulation routines presented in Part III.

Several alternative programs were examined to obtain information about allocations of production, potential investment, and future industry employment levels. Each chapter in Part III is devoted to discussion and analysis of the results of optimizing the linear programming model for a specific construction program and set of constraints. Chapter 6 deals with the outcome of the small program with production rates peaking in the early 1970s and tapering off subsequently. Chapter 7 discusses the results for the large program with peaked production in the early 1970s. In Chapter 8, scheduling is not one of the inputs to the analysis, but becomes an output. An optimal schedule that minimizes the present value of costs is obtained for both the high- and low-production programs.

The effects of maintaining extra capacity in the industry by selectively allocating orders to all shipyards are discussed in Chapter 9. The final analytical chapter is Chapter 10 which analyzes potential investment in new yards. Chapter 11 provides a summary of all the results.

6 The Small Shipbuilder Program with Early Peaking

All the demand problems for a given number of ships that were solved with the linear programming model utilized the same cost-minimizing objective function. The different situations analyzed were characterized by different stipulated values for the constraints under which the firms operated. The small shipbuilding program, with peaked delivery in the early 1970s, required that the majority of the ships be built during the first two of the three 4-year periods over which the model extended. No restrictions were placed on the distribution of orders, labor-force effects, utilization of total capacity, investment in shipyard modernization, and production costs and market prices of ships.

Table 6-1 gives the numbers and types of ships required to be built by the end of each period for the peaked, small-demand program.

6-1 Distribution of Shipbuilding Activity

The construction requirements of the smaller program could be satisfied using only seven yards. An eighth yard is assumed to receive contracts from sources outside the model. The remaining seven yards would not produce any major ships.

Table 6-2 shows the distribution of ships over the seven yards receiving contracts. Only the four lowest cost producers—three of them in the South—

Table 6-1
Ship Demands by Type and Period, Small Program

Ships	Period I	Period II	Period III	Totals
1. DXGN	3	4	3	10
2. DX/DXG	44	66	28	138
3. SSN	7	8	10	25
4. SM URGS	3	3	0	6
5. SM MERCH	36	36	36	108
6. MED AUX	4	5	2	11
7. MED MERCH	24	24	24	72
8. LG URGS	7	3	0	10
9. TANKERS	20	20	20	60

Table 6-2
Ships Awarded by Yard and Period, Small Program

Shipyard	Period I	Period II	Period III	12-Year Totals
Gulf Coast yards				
New yard	39	42	48	129
Yard 1*	—	19	26	45
Yard 2	50	54	13	117
Yard 3	0	0	0	0
East Coast yards				
Yard 4	14	13	0	27
Yard 5	5	0	0	5
Yard 6	32	32	29	93
Yard 7	9	0	0	9
Yard 8	0	0	0	0
Yard 9	0	0	0	0
Yard 10	0	0	0	0
West Coast yards				
Yard 11	0	0	0	0
Yard 12	0	0	0	0
Yard 13	0	0	0	0
Yard 14	0	0	0	0
Regional totals	61	45	29	135
National Totals	150	160	116	426

*In Period I this yard utilized all its capacity to complete present contracts.

would build throughout the dodecade.[1] The new yard, together with another large Southern yard, would build over 50 percent of the ships in the program. All four Western shipyards, plus two of seven in the East and Great Lakes areas, would build no large ships at all. Doubtless, some of these would be engaged in repair, conversion, and the building of smaller ships.

Regional wage differences, which exceed most other cost differentials, explain the comparative advantage which Southern yards enjoy. For example, the labor in Yard 2 in the South is less efficient than that in Yards 4, 5, 6, or 7 in the East. Yet variable cost in Yard 2, after wages are taken into account, is 2 to 6 percent lower on almost all ship types. Only one Eastern yard, producing a limited range of ships, appears capable of producing at costs equal to Yard 2. Pacific Coast shipyards, located in the highest wage area, run a distant third in the cost competition. The cost disadvantage of higher wages is compounded by the fact that they have the most obsolescent equipment and techniques. That these firms do not adopt labor-saving equipment as fast as others can be explained by the risk inherent in their marginal positions.

Our conclusion that the high-wage areas are not competitive differs from that of a study by the Maritime Administration, which observed that Western yards have, in fact, won contracts in the past.[2] Such success might stem from their geographic proximity to certain delivery points. In addition, weather advantages in southern California, not incorporated into the model, could provide productivity offsets for Western yards. On the other hand, more favorable union rules, also excluded from consideration here, prevail in the South. A more likely explanation of past activity in the West is the Navy's post-war policy of spreading procurement over a large number of yards in order to maintain excess capacity. In the absence of such a policy the high-cost yards are unlikely to receive orders, and even at a high level of demand for ships, would operate at lower output rates, relative to their capacity. Thus, they would probably earn lower returns on invested capital than yards where labor is cheaper.

The general-purpose assault ships (LHAs), fast combatant oilers (AOEs), combat store ships (AFSs), and auxiliary ships would be produced in single orders, although the last two types involve quantities of only six ships and two ships, respectively. The guided missile destroyers (DXG) would be built by a single yard, while the destroyers (DD-963 class) would be split between two yards. Submarines are built by two yards. Small merchant ships would be built in a yard in the East and one in the South in runs of 71 and 37 ships, respectively. Larger merchant ships would be distributed among four yards with two runs in the South of 38 and 23 ships, respectively, and two small first-period runs in Eastern yards.

The dominant role played by the new yard within the industry is obvious. Because of its much lower labor costs, especially in steel erection, the new yard can always win sufficient business to fully occupy its assembly and launch facilities. It shows the greatest efficiency in producing ships requiring high proportions of labor relative to materials. This results from the wage advantage it shares with other Southern yards and from the higher productivity of its labor. The new yard also has a comparative advantage in building ships requiring high proportions of steelwork relative to outfitting and electronics work. Its greatest advantage is in building the LHA and AOE.[3] Once the ships for which the new yard is best suited were finished or were to be dropped from the budget, it would acquire orders where its relative cost advantage is smaller but still sufficient to make it the cheapest producer. Because the construction of LHAs, AOEs, and FDLs ends in Period II, new yard capacity becomes available in Periods II and III, attracting awards of large merchant ships and destroyers that in the early period are built elsewhere. The availability of space in the new yard in later periods is the main reason that orders are split.

The splitting of production runs, for a single ship design, raises some questions about the economies related to the cost-progress curve. As we saw in Chapter 4, the average cost of a ship declines as the number of ships produced in a single production run increases. In addition to the learning phenomenon, a programmed high rate of activity motivates a firm to make improvements in facilities which otherwise might not be considered. The decision on whether to split a ship order between a high-cost yard in an early period and a lower-cost yard in a later one hinges upon whether the increased efficiency and lower wage rate of the lower-cost yard is sufficient to offset the diseconomies of breaking the cost-progress curve by splitting a run.

Participation by Litton in a split program would lower total costs of production in certain cases, despite the costs of initiating a second production run. Splitting orders is economic if there are large differences in efficiency between the lower-cost yard and the original producer, and if the number of ships ordered from the lower-cost yard is great enough to take advantage of the learning-curve effects. For instance, if cost-progress rates are equal at both yards, but first-ship cost is 10 percent less in one, then the lower-cost yard must produce at least 56 percent of the entire ship run in order to bring the total program cost below that of producing all ships in the higher-cost yard. If the cost differential is 20 percent, then only 22 percent of the ships need go to the low-cost yard to justify splitting the order.[4]

Use of such percentage terms tends to overstate the precision with which such a splitting decision can be made, however. A run of 15 to 30 ships should be enough to realize most of the economies of learning regardless of the size of total order.[5] In addition, the concept of optimal splitting of orders becomes operational only if the Navy is willing not only to accept bids for different numbers of ships, fractions of the total order, but also to permit the bids to apply to different delivery times. In this way a yard that was operating at capacity could bid for future production. Alternatively, the Navy could attempt to project the production schedules of the low-cost yards and let early bids for some fraction of the total requirement for a given vessel, expecting these to be built by higher-cost yards, and then let contracts for the remainder at a point in time when the low-cost yards are no longer fully employed. Whether the yards or the Navy attempt such long-range cost and production forecasts, however, they are likely to be considerably more uncertain than the solution to our programming problem would imply. Thus, in reality, there may be no sound alternative to letting a single contract all at once and to one yard.

6-2 Labor-Force Changes

Each yard begins the dodecade with a certain collection of skilled labor available. As the yard receives orders, a larger and larger fraction of its labor force is absorbed into construction activities. Once all the men of one skill type are being utilized, the yard must hire and train more, and its costs begin to rise. Any yard with a large amount of business will be adding to its initial labor force. Conversely, if a yard receives little or no business, it will have excess labor that it must get rid of. One assumption made in the analysis, however, was that labor-force adjustments were not instantaneous. At the end of each four-year period a yard's available labor force would be reduced by one-half the number excess to the current requirements. This reduced labor force then comprised the initial labor supply for the next four-year period, and, where applicable, was the base from which the costs of expanding production were calculated.

Table 6-3 shows the pattern of expansion and contraction of labor utilization in the seven active yards. Naturally, this pattern parallels the rate of shipbuilding activity. In the solution for the small program, four of the seven participating yards increase their total employment. Three are in the South and one in the East. These aggregate figures, however, obscure many individual labor market developments. In fact, six of the seven participating yards hire and train new labor for at least one skill at some time; three add labor in all skill groups. One yard hires for two skills, and two hire for only one skill while releasing personnel in other categories. This usually results from imbalance in a yard's initial labor force. If employment data for the base year reflect the start or finish of a shipbuilding program, then satisfaction of the labor requirements for building whole ships over a four-year period means rounding out the skill composition of the labor force. Unbalanced expansion also can be required by a change in the skills needed to build the ships awarded to that yard. Most new hiring takes place in the early 1970s (Period I), reflecting a shift in new shipbuilding to the

Table 6-3
Labor Utilization by Yard and Period, Small Program (Percent of 1967 Labor Force)

Shipyard	Period I	Period II	Period III
Gulf Coast yards			
New Yard	135	124	96
Yard 1	100	115	97
Yard 2	141	144	68
Regional average†	119	118	77
East Coast yards			
Yard 4	90	95	0
Yard 5	79	0	0
Yard 6	145	151	145
Yard 7	46	0	0
Regional average†	60	59	18
National average†	75	72	40

*The new yard's base-year labor force is estimated for 1971.

†The averages encompass all yards in the region whether or not they appear in the table (i.e., build some ships).

most efficient yards as a result of a concentration of orders. Small amounts of new hiring occur in the mid-1970s, but none in the late 1970s. Only one Eastern yard, producing commercial ships with sustained demand, uses more than its initial labor force in the last period. The new yard, while still using its ways time fully, turns to less labor-intensive ships in Period III.

The absolute numbers of idle as well as the newly hired skilled workmen are shown only by region, although expansion and contraction are by no means uniform for all yards within each region. Table 6-4 indicates that overall regional expansion of skilled shipyard employment occurs only in the South. Yet even in this region, although only half of the idle men are assumed to be released, layoffs would overtake new hires by the mid-1970s, and by the end of the 1970s, the early expansion would be completely offset. Labor-force reduction in the South, however, is confined entirely to one yard not producing any major ships. Thus, in the late 1970s (Period III), unemployment would be heavy, even in Southern shipyards. In the East and Great Lakes, where four of seven existing yards receive contracts for major ships, only one yard would hire new labor in sizeable amounts. The decline in skilled employment in the East is about 2,450

Table 6-4
Skilled-labor-force Changes by Region and Period, Small Program

Region	Period I	Period II	Period III	12-year Totals
Gulf Coast				
New hires	3,543	410	0	3,953
Men idle	1,224	1,203	5,778	8,205
Difference	2,319	–793	–5,778	–4,252
Net employment change*	+2,931	–191	–2,889	–149
East Coast				
New hires	642	102	0	744
Men idle	6,186	4,032	6,716	16,934
Difference	–5,544	–3,930	–6,716	–16,190
Net employment change*	–2,451	–1,914	–3,358	–7,723
West Coast				
New hires	–	–	–	–
Men idle	4,227	2,561	1,281	8,069
Difference	–4,227	–2,561	–1,281	–8,069
New employment change*	–2,113	–1,281	–641	–4,035
Total				
New hires	4,185	512	0	4,697
Men idle	11,637	7,700	13,775	33,208
Difference	–7,452	–7,284	–13,775	–28,511
Net employment change*	–1,633	–3,386	–6,888	–11,907

men in Period I, 1,900 men in Period II, and 3,350 men in Period III: a total of 7,700 from an original skilled employment level of 13,300. Western yards would not participate in building major ships.

For the nation as a whole the level of demand generated by the small-order program, coupled with the consolidation of orders, yields a highly localized contraction of shipyard employment. (This result will be contrasted later in Chapter 9 with the projected effects of a policy of deliberate work dispersion.) A large part of the reduction in labor force takes place in the first period. (See Table 6-4.) There is a possibility that some of the first-period contraction could be offset by new hiring in other yards and regions. Because the number of idle employees remains fairly high in the mid-1970s, while the number of new hires falls sharply, the net rate of employment contraction increases with time. If half of the idle men are laid off in each period, over 15,000 skilled workers would become unemployed over the 12 years, and skilled employment in the industry would shrink by a net figure of 11,900: 1,600 in Period I, 3,400 in Period II, and 6,900 in Period III. Unskilled personnel would be laid off in addition. Yet, despite all laying off there still would be idle workers in the yards at the end of the period. Whether or not the skilled workers rendered unemployed (e.g., electricians, sheet metal workers, and other outfitting workers) would be able to find jobs in the construction, aircraft, and other industries would depend upon the level of activity in those industries. Their skills would be more transferable than certain hull-erection workers (e.g., shipwrights).

6-3 Ways-Capacity Utilization

The capacity of a productive facility derives from an aggregate of factors difficult to define or measure. The concept used here is a percentage of ways space or time used. Thus, when a yard uses one-half of its building positions or uses all of them only half the time, it operates at 50 percent of its "capacity."

Table 6-5 shows our estimates of the percentage of capital capacity utilized in various yards over the three time periods. Only Litton and one Eastern yard would fully use their building positions throughout the dodecade. One other Southern yard is almost fully utilized. Two more yards, one each in the South and the East, would be fully or heavily occupied for two periods, but nearly idle in the third period. Two Eastern firms, the least active yards participating, provide only marginal facilities in the earliest period.

The percentage of ways utilization in certain instances varies inversely in relation to labor utilization from one period to the next. This variation results from a shift to building ships which require different amounts of labor, relative to ways time. For example, while commercial ships require roughly the same amount of time at a building position as many naval ships, they use less labor per

Table 6-5
Capacity Utilization by Yard and Period, Small Program (Percent of Available Ways Time)*

Shipyard	I	II	III
Gulf Coast			
New Yard	100	100	100
Yard 1	100†	86	100
Yard 2	92	97	26
Regional average‡	78	86	56
East Coast			
Yard 4	100	100	0
Yard 5	11	0	0
Yard 6	100	100	100
Yard 7	26	0	0
Regional average‡	28	21	5
National average‡	44	41	27

*The time on ways stipulated for each ship represents "normal" practice for well-employed yards.

†Yard 1's utilization in Period I is set outside the model.

‡The averages encompass all yards in the region, whether or not they appear in the table.

ways per month. Therefore, whenever a yard increases production of merchant ships relative to that of naval ships (as do the more efficient yards in the later periods), labor utilization drops substantially, even though ways utilization changes very little. Production in the new yard, for example, is predominantly naval ships in Period II (83 percent of its total) but is merchant ships and destroyers in Period III. While merchant ships require less labor, destroyers require more time on the ways than the ships that the yard was building previously. Thus, although the ways continue to be fully occupied, labor utilization drops by almost one-quarter.

6-4 Investments in Shipyard Modernization

The amount of investment in new equipment is projected simultaneously with production activity. Table 6-6 shows by region the values of equipment outlays which result from the small shipbuilding program. The first line shows the total budget outlay over the dodecade. To make the expenditure streams comparable, present values, discounted at 10 percent, also are shown. The dollar values given for investment include only the manufacturer's sale price of selected items. Installation or start-up costs would vary greatly among yards and cannot be generalized accurately. Thus, the investment values shown below considerably understate the full cost of modernizing the shipyards.

Table 6-6
Value of Equipment Purchases by Region, Small Program ($ millions)

	Gulf Coast Yards	East Coast Yards	West Coast Yards	Total
Undiscounted values	1.15	1.15	0	2.30
Discounted values (at 10 percent)	.90	1.14	0	2.04

Since the four Western yards do not build major ships in this program, none would find it profitable to modernize equipment. Four East Coast yards could win contracts, and only two of these that operate throughout the period would find it profitable to fully modernize their equipment. Investment on the Gulf Coast would also occur in two yards. Thus, under the small program, the industry would have four completely modernized yards on the Gulf and East Coasts, in addition to the new yard. As for the construction of entirely new shipyard capacity, the analysis indicates that no such investments would be profitable with the small demand. (See Chapter 10.)

6-5 Shipyard Production Costs vs. Prices to the Buyers

The ship costs that determine the allocation of orders are the sums of shipyard production costs. These are functions not only of the amount of inputs used per ship but also of the level of production in the yard. The costs are related but certainly not equivalent to the price the buyers pay. The assumption of competitive bidding on a production run equal to the total demand for each ship type implies that a unique price exists for each kind of ship. This uniform price tends to approach the marginal ship cost in the least efficient operating yard. The total cost to the buyers of a particular ship type would be the product of the number of ships times the price. This will exceed the total variable production cost of building the ships. The difference is the return on investment in yards more efficient than the marginal yard.

Estimates of the winning bid prices for all ship categories are calculated as part of the solution to the linear program. These are the "shadow prices" associated with the demand constraints. Using these prices it is possible to compare the cost to buyers of a particular shipbuilding program with the production costs of the yards.

For the small program, the discounted present value of the entire program's production cost is $7.6 billion.[6] The present value of the customer's cost, at $8.0 billion, is only about 5 percent higher. The corresponding undiscounted values—which might be called the projected budget costs—are $10.0 billion and $10.5 billion, respectively, for 12 years. Thus, the difference between producers' and customers' costs is remarkably small. Were the program larger or the cost curves steeper, the difference would increase.

If, contrary to the premise of a competitive market, a dominant buyer (in this case the U.S. government) exercised its power by playing one builder against another, it might obtain some ships at prices closer to their variable production costs. In this case, however, the gains from doing so would be limited to the 5 percent differentials discussed in the previous paragraph. Moreover, appropriation of this return to efficient capital by the buyer would have serious consequences in deterring future investment in the industry. In effect, it would lead eventually to the decline of the industry through deterioration of capital which causes variable costs to rise.

As the rate of shipbuilding decreases in the later 1970s, the bid prices of ships for new orders would presumably decline because fewer of the high-cost firms are required to produce them. Thus, marginal facilities (on which the price is based) would be more efficient than those operating earlier in the decade. The effect that production rate has on real resource inputs can be examined by looking at undiscounted marginal costs (ship shadow prices). These decline by 5 to 10 percent between the initial and the final period. This difference is small and reflects again the small size of the program.

7 A Large Shipbuilding Program

The large simulated shipbuilding program represented an increase over the small one of slightly less than 100 percent in the total number of ships required by 1980. The number of merchant ships and tankers is more than doubled, which accounts for the major part of the increase. Submarines (SSOs) are added to the Period III demand, and the destroyer program is increased by 30 percent. In addition, a sizeable FDL program is included. Delivery requirements peak in the first four years and gradually decline subsequently.

7-1 Distribution of Shipbuilding Activity

This program requires all 15 yards in the model to build ships during the first four-year period, whereas only seven firms participated in the small program. One of the 15 receives its contracts externally rather than as part of the analysis. Under the large program, these seven yards, plus one in the West, build during all periods, as seen in Table 7-2. Although the work is now spread more widely among regions, there are, nevertheless, three yards without contracts in the mid-1970s and six yards without work in the late 1970s. This is in contrast, however, to the 10 yards that become idle in the small program.

The four lowest-cost yards produce about the same number of ships as in the small program because they again operate at their maximum rate of output.

Table 7-1
Ship Demands by Type and Period, Large Program

Ships	Period I	Period II	Period III	Totals
1. DXGN	4	3	3	10
2. DX/DXG	57	73	36	166
3. SSN	7	8	15	30
4. SM URGS	3	3	–	6
5. SM MERCH	76	76	76	228
6. MED AUX	4	5	2	11
7. MED MERCH	52	52	52	156
8. LC URGS	7	3	–	10
9. TANKER	60	60	60	180

Table 7-2
Ships Awarded by Yard and Period, Large Program

Shipyard	Period I	Period II	Period III	12-year Totals
New yard	39	41	48	128
Other Gulf yards				
Yard 1*	–	22	22	44
Yard 2	52	52	60	164
Yard 3	5	3	0	8
Regional totals	96	118	130	344
East Coast yards				
Yard 4	14	17	16	47
Yard 5	53	53	31	137
Yard 6	26	28	31	85
Yard 7	28	28	23	79
Yard 8	7	0	0	7
Yard 9	10	7	0	17
Yard 10*	17	0	0	17
Regional totals	155	133	101	389
West Coast yards				
Yard 11	20	20	0	40
Yard 12*	6	16	12	34
Yard 13	14	0	0	14
Yard 14	4	0	0	4
Regional totals	44	36	12	92
National totals	295	287	243	825

*These yards utilize some or all initial capacity in Period I for completing present contracts not included in this program.

These four yards win orders for about 50 percent of the total number of ships, and as a result of the increase in demand for each type of ship, they build longer runs of the ships in which their relative advantage is the greatest. Thus, they do not switch to the construction of other types of ships in the later periods. With the large demand, more specialization occurs in all yards.

As before, the general-purpose assault ships (LHAs) and fast combatant oilers (AOEs) are produced in single orders in the new yard. Now the FDLs are produced there as well, whereas combat store ships (AFSs) are produced together, but in another yard. The destroyer and associated guided-missle destroyer programs are again divided among three yards. Construction of nuclear frigates and submarines is shared by two yards. Small merchant ships are split among nine producers. None, however, produces for more than two periods, a consequence of a shift in production in later periods to more efficient yards as capacity becomes available. The large contracts, for 46 and 40 ships, respectively, are awarded early in the decade; two others, for 47 and 34 ships, are placed in the mid-1970s. Six yards build the large merchant ships, with the four largest orders being for 51, 44, 27, and 19 ships. Two small orders for merchant ships are placed with marginal facilities in the first period, because the heavy demand for ships uses full capacity of more efficient yards.

Many of the results of the simulated small program hold for the large program as well. The lowest-cost yards are initially filled to capacity with ships for which they have the greatest cost advantage. As they complete these ships, they begin production of others, while less efficient yards become idle. As in the small program, the new yard shifts in Periods II and III from large noncombatant military ships to destroyers and merchant ships. The six highest-cost yards receive orders for merchant ships and tankers only during the early periods when total demand exceeds the capacity of the efficient yards.

7-2 Labor-Force Changes

Referring to Table 7-3, we see that rapid labor-force expansion takes place in many yards. Six firms, in contrast to only one in the small program, retain more skilled workers throughout the late 1970s than they had in the base year. These six are evenly divided between South and East.

In the South, three of four yards expand their employment during the first two periods, and two of these continue their growth throughout the last period. All but two Eastern yards take on additional labor. During this same period of the early 1970s, the rate of expansion in the East (and the Great Lakes) almost equals that of the South. In later periods, however, Eastern expansion is reversed, while Southern yards continue to grow.

Two Western yards expand initially but drop below their 1967 employment levels in the middle period. Declining employment is due to only one or two Western yards' building major ships at all after Period I. One Western yard, however, survives in good economic health throughout the decade.

Nine yards operate at one time or another with over 30 percent more labor than in 1967. This implies that they build ships at costs more than 7 percent above their minimum levels. The conspicuous case of Yard 5, which increases its employment fivefold, is explained in that expansion beyond 160 percent of base-year labor use can continue at the same cost to the limit of production set by the ways. Moreover, Yard 5 has a small labor force in its base year, relative to its extensive ways facilities. Of the several yards qualified to build merchant ships of all types, this yard is among the low-cost ones, and the full utilization of its capital is, therefore, a logical choice over expansion in other available yards.

Table 7-4 shows labor-market developments in absolute numbers of men by

Table 7-3
Labor Utilization by Yard and Period, Large Program (Percents of 1967 Labor Force)

Yard	Period I	Period II	Period III
Gulf Coast			
New Yard	146	128	96
Yard 1	102	139	139
Yard 2	175	193	202
Yard 3	87	42	0
Regional average	144	144	130
East Coast			
Yard 4	65	74	81
Yard 5	562	560	267
Yard 6	183	178	163
Yard 7	171	171	120
Yard 8	76	0	0
Yard 9	175	110	0
Yard 10	127	0	0
Regional average	139	106	77
West Coast			
Yard 11	89	89	0
Yard 12	142	96	75
Yard 13	131	0	0
Yard 14	95	0	0
Regional average	109	59	14
National Average	136	114	89

region. Even the large program leaves many workers idle in later periods. If we assume again that half of the unnecessary men are released in each period, the industry as a whole shows a net expansion of over 2,000 skilled men for the decade. A certain complement of semiskilled and unskilled workers would be hired in addition.

The number of layoffs within each region shows clearly the course of the industry's fortunes in that region over the decade. As with the small program, the three regions fare differently, with the South leading in prosperity. Only Southern yards would employ more men in 1980 than in 1967, expanding by some 5,000 skilled men or by about 40 percent. The Eastern yards as a group expand sharply in the early 1970s, but return to slightly under their original employment by 1980. The West also expands in Period I, but by the end of the 1970s it has laid off almost 60 percent of its 1967 skilled labor. Indeed, as seen

Table 7-4
Skilled-labor-force Expansion and Contraction by Region and Period, Large Program

Region	I	Period II	III	12-year Totals
Gulf Coast				
New hires	5,615	1,493	610	7,718
Men idle	415	1,712	3,249	5,378
Difference	5,200	−1,219	−2,639	2,342
Net employment change*	5,407	637	−1,015	5,030
East Coast				
New hires	7,430	14	175	7,619
Men idle	2,979	5,847	6,957	15,783
Difference	4,451	−5,833	−6,782	−8,164
Net employment change*	5,940	−2,910	−3,304	−273
West Coast				
New hires	728	1	0	729
Men idle	678	2,722	3,421	6,821
Difference	50	−2,721	−3,421	−6,092
Net employment change*	389	−1,360	−1,711	−2,682
Totals				
New hires	13,773	1,508	785	16,066
Men idle	4,072	10,281	13,627	27,980
Difference	9,701	−8,773	−12,842	−11,914
Net employment change*	11,737	−3,633	−6,029	2,076

*Half of the idled workers are assumed to be laid off in each period.

in Table 7-3, Western yards in the last period actually put to use only 14 percent, on the average, of their 1967 labor force.

7-3 Ways-Capacity Utilization

Ways capacity is fully utilized throughout the decade in five yards, as seen in Table 7-5. In two other yards, the ways capacity is fully employed, except for a minor slump in the final period, and in another, the capacity is used at a high rate throughout all years. Thus, eight yards make heavy use of their capital facilities, in contrast to the small program, where only two yards are fully utilized and two others are partially occupied throughout all periods. Under the large program, at least one or possibly two of the four existing Western yards would prosper. It is interesting that they fare better than one Southern yard and

Table 7-5
Capacity Utilization by Yard and Period, Large Program (Percent of 1967 Ways Time)

Shipyard	Period I	Period II	Period III
Gulf Coast			
New yard	100	100	100
Yard 1	100	100	100
Yard 2	100	100	100
Yard 3	17	11	0
Regional average	88	86	85
East Coast			
Yard 4	100	100	100
Yard 5	100	100	56
Yard 6	100	100	100
Yard 7	86	86	68
Yard 8	24	0	0
Yard 9	96	65	0
Yard 10*		n.a.	
Regional average	83	76	55
West Coast			
Yard 11	100	100	0
Yard 12	100	100	87
Yard 13	81	0	0
Yard 14	76	0	0
Regional average	95	60	19
National Average†	87	78	63

*This yard receives a sizable amount of business not incorporated into the model.

†Yard 10 is excluded–both from utilization in the model and from total regional and national capacity.

two yards in the Eastern group, despite the substantial wage advantages in these regions. This is attributed to relative technical efficiency.

One may wonder why certain firms, Yards 7 and 9, for example, operating at high production rates are not pushed to their maximum utilization before orders spill over into the marginal yards. As we see from the labor-utilization rates in Table 7-3, these yards use more than their initial labor endowments and therefore operate at rates of production where their per-unit costs increase. There are several potential reasons for their failure to win the few additional ship orders needed to utilize their remaining capacity. It is possible that they encounter a constraint on the rate of employment expansion at this point which would raise the costs of further production above the costs at which competitors can fulfill the orders. Alternatively, it may be that having fully satisfied the demand for the ship types in which their comparative advantage lies, they cannot compete successfully for other ships. Finally, it may be that some of the yards' ways remain unused because they are too small to accommodate the type of ships needed.

In conclusion, it should be noted that an optimally allocated shipbuilding program of this magnitude would sustain capacity to build major ships in each coastal area of the country without the need for additional subsidies. As a result of their high activity rates, the 9 or 10 producing yards should have sufficient incentive to modernize and maintain their facilities. If such modernization were to be a national objective, however, there are much cheaper ways of achieving it than to embark on a large shipbuilding program. The likelihood exists, moreover, that a program of this size would make profitable the construction of additional new yards, which would undercut some existing yards and alter considerably the geographical distribution of capacity.

7-4 Investment in Yard Modernization

The heavy demand for ships induces several shipyards on the Gulf and East Coasts to undertake thorough modernization of their equipment. Four of the yards exhaust their potential opportunities for equipment replacement. (The new yard is considered to be completely modern at the outset.) The yards, in these regions, which are least well equipped at the outset would fail to invest. In the West, one yard makes all possible investments, while two others exercise most of the investment options. The remaining Western yard makes only about one-quarter of its potential investments. Table 7-6 displays the values of investment aggregated by region. These values include only the purchase price of the equipment.

Because ship delivery requirements are very heavy in the early 1970s under this program, all investment takes place during the first four-year period. Clearly it is in the interests of yards producing throughout the decade to invest immediately to enjoy the maximum potential cost savings. Moreover, the industry's capacity is heavily strained during the early years. Eighty-seven percent of total ways time is used in Period I and 78 percent in Period II. No

Table 7-6
The Value of Equipment Purchases by Region,* Large Program ($ million)

Gulf Coast	East Coast	West Coast	Total
$1.65	$4.96	$2.59	$9.20

*Because all investments take place in Period I, discounted values are not shown.

fewer than eight yards operate at full utilization during both these periods. Four others exceed 75 percent utilization. With such high activity rates in the industry, investments are also warranted for the expansion in capital which they would bring. This level of demand, therefore, is sufficient to warrant the replacement during Period I of about three-quarters (by value) of the obsolete equipment owned by the industry.

Over 50 percent of the value of investments in Southern and Western yards would go to increase the lift capability of the yards' cranes. In the East, only 30 percent would be devoted to this purpose. In all regions, most of the remainder would be spent for numerical fairing and lofting equipment. Only a small proportion would be used to purchase improved steel handling and processing machinery. Recent advances in this phase of shipbuilding have already been incorporated into most active yards.

As elaborated in Chapter 10, the construction of additional new yards under the large shipbuilding program would both increase total industry investment and preempt some of the piecemeal modernization of existing yards envisioned here.

7-5 The Level of Production Costs and Prices for the Large Program

The present value of the production cost for the large shipbuilding program (with future costs discounted at 10 percent per year) is \$13.7 billion (in 1968 dollars). This figure is 80 percent higher than that for the smaller program. The present value of the aggregate cost of the program to the customers, calculated using ship shadow prices, is \$15.5 billion. This is 13 percent greater than the variable production costs, as compared with a 5 percent difference in the small program. The greater difference in the large program results from many less efficient yards producing ships, thereby yielding higher marginal costs (shadow prices) for additional ships. Eventual outlays (undiscounted) by the producers would be about \$18 billion, or \$1.67 billion per year.

The increase in demand under the larger program raises the bid prices of ships by between 8 and 29 percent as compared to the small program. The additional ships must be built at higher, more costly production rates in efficient yards or in altogether higher-cost yards. The greatest difference occurs during the first two periods when the industry reaches its peak building rate. The ships for which price differences are the greatest are commercial ships (tankers, container-ships, and cargo liners). The optimal allocation of these ships among yards is the most easily affected by the volume of activity. Prices fall, however, toward the end of the period. The decline in activity in the large program between the early and late 1970s brings about a 9 to 27 percent decline from the peak prices, depending on the ship. For the reasons cited above, tanker prices fall by around

23 percent, large merchant ships and destroyers by about 20 percent, and submarines and nuclear ships by only 10 percent.

8 Smoothing the Production Schedule

As emphasized earlier, this study projects the costs and simulates the allocation decisions for two arbitrary sets of ship demands. It makes no generalizations about the number of ships needed nor the timing of these needs. A thorough analysis of costs, however, should consider whether significant savings can be achieved by eliminating specific fleet requirements in early years and permitting the delivery schedule to become an internal decision, variable rather than arbitrarily fixed. If the total demand for a fleet of ships is stated as of 1980 with no earlier delivery schedule stipulated, it is possible, using an appropriate objective function, to schedule shipbuilding to achieve maximum technical and organizational efficiency with minimum amounts of physical resources.

The choice of an optimal production time schedule to satisfy some fixed output requirement inevitably depends upon the alternative uses to which the real resources involved can be put, assuming there is excess capacity. With no excess capacity, any alternatives are irrelevant, but this is certainly not the case in shipbuilding. If the resources required for some project are sufficiently malleable so that they could equally well be used in another activity, the potential return of the alternative use must enter into the production decision for the project being considered.

Thus, suppose a firm owned a plant that could produce alternatively ball bearings or roller skates, and it had an order to be delivered by the end of the year for a quantity of ball bearings equal to one-half the plant's annual capacity. It could produce the total order operating at its full output capacity for one half year or half capacity for a full year or use any combination of time and operating capacity that it wished. Assume further that its daily operating costs at full production are identical for either product and that it receives payment for output on delivery even though the contract date for the ball bearings is the last day of December.

Given the conditions we have postulated, there are only two logical scheduling alternatives the firm might consider, assuming the return that can be earned on receipts is positive. If a day's production of roller skates sells for more than a day's production of ball bearings, the ball-bearing production would be postponed to the second half of the year. The converse would be true if a day's output of ball bearings was worth more than that of roller skates. The decision is independent of any kind of alternative rate of return in the economy as a whole, and it is a decision that maximizes the present value of the *firm's* earnings.

Suppose now the plant is specific for the production of ball bearings and that no alternative product exists. If there are no startup or shutdown costs and if the firm can be indifferent about the work patterns of its personnel, it would still prefer to produce everything during the first half of the year and close down during the second half. These conditions are unlikely to hold, however. Startup costs may be significant, and wide swings in employment can be costly to the firm as well as to the people involved. Given a choice in the matter, the firm would probably find that the optimal production path is the one that smooths out production over the year or any longer period it might be operating. Such a conclusion would undoubtedly be correct for a firm contemplating new investment in order to satisfy a given long-term demand. Stable output would enable it to choose an optimal size plant and thus minimize its investment and unit costs. The conclusion is less tenable if the investment is already in place and the stable output level is less than capacity. But even in this case, the problems associated with large fluctuations in hiring may make it more desirable to stabilize production.

The desirability of stabilizing output is the rationale that underlies the objective function used to choose an optimal ship delivery schedule and in measuring the cost of such a schedule. The actual ship costs contained in the analysis were unchanged from those used earlier, but no discounting of future costs was permitted nor were any measures of potential earnings on early receipts considered. If the values of resources used can be considered as surrogates for the quantities of real resources, then such a procedure minimizes the amount of physical resources needed to build a given number of ships over the 12-year period. In the absence of alternatives for the capital assets required and, given the apparent uncertainty of alternatives for the labor, this is a defensible social as well as private goal, if the cost savings make up for whatever inconvenience may accrue to purchasers of ships due to the change in delivery schedules.

Somewhat surprisingly, freedom of production scheduling, while it avoids much dislocation of labor, would yield only negligible cost savings (less than 1 percent) for the total program. This occurs despite economies in hiring and investment and exploitation of some additional "learning" possibilities. Reduced production rates and prices in the first period are offset by increases in the last period, and some of the costs of expanding the labor force are incurred anyway.

Table 8-1 shows the orders and rates of resource utilization for the small program, and Table 8-2 presents the large program. Comparing Table 8-1 with Table 6-2, we see that two yards which had won small orders in Period I under the stipulated delivery schedule can no longer compete. Thus, the small program is now carried out in only five yards, all working at high production rates, especially in the last two periods.

On the other hand, 12 yards participate in the large program (Table 8-1). Of these, 11 operate at more than 50 percent utilization of their ways time, while 7, including 2 in the West, employ full capacity throughout the decade. Two

Table 8-1
Ships Awarded and Percent of Initial Yard Resources Utilized by Period with Optimal Production Scheduling, Small Program

	Number of Ships				Ways Utilization			Labor Utilization		
	Period			12-year	Period			Period		
Shipyard	I	II	III	Totals	I	II	III	I	II	III
Gulf Coast										
New yard	39	42	48	129	100	100	100	118	118	118
Yard 1	–	23	23	46	100	100	100	100	121	121
Yard 2	21	41	42	104	46	81	83	116	136	136
Regional total (averages)	60	106	113	279	(63)	(75)	(76)	(103)	(113)	(113)
East Coast										
Yard 4	19	18	18	55	100	100	100	65	65	65
Yard 6	23	33	33	89	81	100	100	117	119	119
Regional total (averages)	42	51	51	144	(21)	(22)	(22)	(39)	(40)	(40)
National total (averages)	102	157	164	423	(36)	(43)	(43)	(59)	(64)	(64)

marginal yards, which were included when early delivery of ships was required, now drop out of the solution. Elimination of marginal yards occurs because early requirements can be postponed, allowing the more efficient yards to satisfy demands at a later date rather than calling on higher-cost yards to build during Period I.

Under both programs the utilization of ways would increase over time in yards not initially operating at full capacity. This gradual increase reflects an orderly expansion of operations, contrasting sharply with the hasty response to the surge in demands described in Chapters 6 and 7. Although the total costs are little affected, this smoother output schedule has an important influence on the activities of the industry. All firms which produce in the first period continue to produce at equal or higher utilization rates in later periods, and no investment or hiring is undertaken which is not fully exploited throughout subsequent years. For both the large and small programs labor expansion is undertaken at a less frenetic pace. Even some of the yards that experience full utilization of ways under both delivery schedules employ less labor in early periods with optimal scheduling and would build up their manpower over time. This results because they are able to use less labor during the earlier years and postpone more labor-intensive ships until the labor-force build-up is completed. As one might predict, the highest level of employment expansion in both programs is typically less than with uneven production schedules. Thus, the same number of ships can be built in fewer yards with lower maximum employment levels.

Table 8-2
Ships Awarded and Percent of Initial Yard Resources Utilized by Period with Optimal Production Scheduling, Large Program

	Number of Ships				Ways Utilization			Labor Utilization		
	Period			12-year	Period			Period		
Shipyard	I	II	III	Totals	I	II	III	I	II	III
Gulf Coast										
New yard	39	43	47	129	100	100	100	121	130	130
Yard 1	–	22	22	44	100	100	100	112	125	125
Yard 2	59	51	51	161	100	100	100	160	183	183
Yard 3	2	2	2	6	7	7	7	28	28	28
Regional total (averages)	100	118	122	340	(86)	(86)	(86)	(125)	(138)	(138)
East Coast										
Yard 4	14	13	13	40	100	100	100	101	101	101
Yard 5	42	41	41	124	74	75	76	339	402	434
Yard 6	31	28	28	87	100	100	100	152	165	165
Yard 7	25	28	28	81	74	86	86	136	170	170
Yard 9	6	7	7	20	52	62	62	92	110	110
Yard 10*	0	0	0	0	n.a.	n.a.	n.a.	100	100	100
Regional total (averages)	118	117	117	352	(65)	(68)	(68)	(125)	(135)	(137)
West Coast										
Yard 11	20	20	20	60	100	100	100	88	88	88
Yard 12	9	16	16	41	100	100	100	102	96	96
Yard 13	11	12	12	35	61	70	70	99	113	113
Regional total (averages)	40	48	48	136	(80)	(83)	(83)	(83)	(88)	(88)
National total (averages)	256	281	285	822	(70)	(71)	(71)	(105)	(115)	(116)

*Yard 10 receives some orders outside of the model.

Table 8-3 indicates that for the large program with freedom of scheduling, certain large ship orders can be consolidated into fewer production runs, and greater specialization by ship type can take place within yards. Such consolidation yields savings through the learning effect and economies associated with longer production runs. Although shown here only for the large program, the same pattern emerges in the smaller one.

The production schedule derived here minimizes the use of physical resources for shipbuilding. Table 8-4 summarizes the labor-force changes for the industry. As a basis for comparison, the totals for the peaked delivery schedule are repeated. To produce the small program, about 1,850 (or 40 percent) fewer

Table 8-3
A Comparison of Ship Orders and Yard Activities for the Smoothed Production Schedules and Large Program

Ship Type	No. of Participating Yards Peaked	No. of Participating Yards Smoothed	Shipyard	No. of Ship Types Produced Peaked	No. of Ship Types Produced Smoothed
1	2	2	New Yard	5	5
2	3	3	1	1	1
3	3	1	2	3	3
4	1	1	3	4	3
5	9	7	4	2	1
6	2	1	5	5	3
7	6	4	6	1	1
8	1	1	7	2	1
9	1	1	8	2	2
10	4	3	9	1	1
			10	1	0
			11	2	1
			12	1	1
			13	1	0
			14	2	2

Table 8-4
Skilled-labor-force Expansion and Contraction with Smoothed Production Rates

Program Size	Period I	Period II	Period III	Total Smoothed	Total Peaked
Small program					
New hires	1,797	1,049	0	2,846	4,697
Men idle	12,905	7,469	3,612	23,987	33,208
Difference	−5,555	−6,420	−3,612	−21,141	−28,511
Net employment change*	−11,108	−3,211	−1,807	−10,570	−11,907
Large program					
New hires	7,733	2,861	253	10,847	16,066
Men idle	6,207	2,701	1,642	10,549	27,980
Difference	+1,526	+160	−1,389	+298	−11,914
Net employment change*	+4,630	+1,510	−568	+5,572	+2,076

*It is assumed that half of the men idle are laid off during each period.

newly hired skilled workers are needed with smooth production rates than with peaks in scheduling. Some 5,200 (or 33 percent) fewer are needed in the large program. At the same time, however, a much smaller number of workers are counted as idle, for none are hired in the early years only to become unemployed later. A larger part of the initial work force is also needed for production in the late 1970s. In short, since the work is extended over a longer time period, the labor force is stabilized and massive reductions in the late 1970s are avoided.

Aggregate investments would be lower because only the most efficient yards are needed to satisfy the demand. These yards already have acquired most available labor-saving equipment and thus would not require as much investment to upgrade their facilities. Because production rises consistently over time, some of these yards would find it profitable to make certain additional investments in Period II which were not warranted in Period I.

9 Contract Dispersal Policies

The results obtained from the shipbuilding programs analyzed in the previous chapters indicate that several shipyards capable of building large ships would receive no contracts after the mid-1970s. A logical conclusion is that these yards would probably close in the absence of a definite government policy designed to keep them in business. There are those in the industry and elsewhere who would argue that such closure would in some way be contrary to national policy objectives. The main argument used to justify the continued support and operation of inefficient shipyards is that they are necessary in terms of their potential contribution toward national defense.

9-1 Costs of Mobilization

As with any military organization, the Navy faces the problem of how best to satisfy a sudden increase in demand for its services. Basically there are four alternatives. The first is to maintain a large fleet, not only of ships, but also of the complementary elements including personnel and supplies. The second is to maintain the ships but not the complements with a large number of ships being stored. The third option is to retain a small fleet of ships and simply to plan on expanding production capacity, when and if it is needed. The fourth alternative is to have a small fleet but maintain sufficient shipyard capacity to be able to increase production rapidly with relatively little capital expenditure. A complete analysis of all four alternatives is beyond the scope of this study, but it is possible to make a partial comparison between the costs of the third and fourth choices.

There are numerous policies that could be used to maintain production facilities, including direct subsidies, but the most politically feasible is to allocate orders so that most yards, regardless of their degree of efficiency, receive a sufficient amount of work to stay in business. There are several elements of cost that would need to be taken into account in examining a decision to deliberately maintain inefficient yards in business. Some of these will be discussed later. For the moment, however, we shall be concerned only with the increase in the cost of building a given collection of ships, since this is the direct budget cost and the only cost that lends itself to estimation, using the analytical apparatus we have developed.

There is no unique allocation policy that the government might wish to adopt. Any policy involves some trade-off between maintaining efficiency and maintaining a total level of productive capacity. In the absence of an optimal mobilization policy, it was possible, nevertheless, to estimate some costs for what might be considered feasible alternatives. These potentially feasible policies were different for the small shipbuilding program and for the large program. For the small program the policies considered were:[1]

1. Maintain all yards in production at equal fractions of total ways capacity.
2. Permit the most efficient yard to operate at full capacity, and allocate the rest of the demand equally across all remaining yards.
3. Permit the two most efficient yards to operate at full capacity, and allocate the rest of the demand equally across all the remaining yards.

For the large program the alternatives considered were:

4. Maintain all yards at equal fractions of total ways capacity.
5. Permit the three most efficient yards to operate at full capacity and allocate the rest of the demand equally across the remaining yards.
6. Set a minimum production rate for each yard of 30 percent in the first period, 23 percent in the second, and 15 percent in the third period.

A policy of maintaining all yards, producing at equal fractions of capacity, would be the most costly for both programs. Not only would all the inefficient yards be used, but even the most efficient yards would have considerable excess capacity. No yard would operate at its optional output or take full advantage of the economies of learning. If production were spread less uniformly, with efficient yards operating at capacity and all others maintained at a smaller proportion of capacity than the equalizing proportion, the direct production costs would be likely to be less, while at the same time the potential mobilization capacity would be less as well, since there almost certainly would be some level of production below which a yard would prefer to go out of business.

The cost differentials that result from each mobilization policy are shown in Table 9-1. The first heading gives the minimum fraction of total ways capacity at each yard which is utilized under the work-dispersion constraints specified above. Heading 2 is the percent increase in costs due to performing the work in the higher cost yards. These estimates do not include the cost attributable to allocating the orders in smaller lots, which is shown under heading 3. The total cost increases appear under heading 4.

For a small program, the price to the government of keeping all yards operating at the same rate is about 9 percent greater than the price of producing the ships without these restrictions. The differential is calculated as a percentage of the price of the small shipbuilding program to the buyers. In budgetary terms,

Table 9-1
Estimated Cost of Maintaining a Mobilization Capability

Policy*	(1) Minimum Capacity Utilization by Period (percent) I	II	III	(2) Cost of Dispersal to High-cost Yards (percent)†	(3) Estimated Small Order Cost (percent)†	(4) Total Added Cost [Columns (2) + (3)] (percent)†	($ mil/year)
Smaller program							
(1)	40	40	26	6.1	3.1	9.2	80
(2)	31	31	16	3.8	0.8	3.0	[illegible]
(3)	19	19	14.5	2.0	0.2	2.2	19
Larger program							
(4)	82	70	56	3.1	1.0	4.1	69
(5)	70	55	34	1.1	0.2	1.3	22
(6)	30	23	15	0.2	0.0	0.2	3

*Policy alternatives are those listed on pages 87.

†The bill to the buyers (undiscounted) when yards are not constrained to a minimum operating level is estimated to average $875 million per year for the smaller program and $1.7 billion for the larger program.

this increase averages about $80 million per year. If one efficient yard produces at capacity and the remainder of the orders are evenly spread, the total difference in variable costs falls to 3 percent. When two efficient yards are permitted to work at full capacity and the rest of the demand is allocated equally among the remaining yards, the cost differential for the small program drops to about 2 percent, or some $19 million annually. It is doubtful, however, that the remaining yards would continue production, utilizing only 19 percent of capacity without additional subsidies. A selective approach probably would have to be applied which would not attempt to dispense work to every yard.

The cost differentials given in Table 9-1 almost certainly understate the total cost increase due to dispersing orders, for two main reasons. First, the more shipyards that are kept in business, the greater the total amount of overhead costs that must be met. These overhead costs are not included in the analysis. Second, once it becomes evident that the government is following a deliberate policy of keeping yards in business, there is little incentive for any of the shipyards to be very competitive in their pricing policies. The inefficient yards, knowing they would receive orders anyway, will price so they cover all costs and make a profit. And thus, the efficient ones will be provided with an umbrella under which they can raise their prices.

With the large program, there is a greater number of yards and a greater fraction of total capacity being utilized, even without spreading orders. Thus, the extra cost of maintaining any given utilization rate in the less efficient yards is lower than for the small program. For example, the additional cost of a policy of equal allocation across yards is about 4 percent greater than the total cost of unrestricted allocation for the same number of ships, or about $70 million per year. A policy of work-spreading is both less costly and less necessary when the volume of business is large enough to occupy all yards.

The appropriate alternative for comparison under the large program, however, is not just that of optimal allocation of orders across existing yards. As will be seen in Chapter 10, the large program makes it profitable to build another large efficient yard equivalent to the Litton yard. If this were done, it would certainly put many of the existing yards out of business, just as Litton theoretically does under the small program. If a work-spreading policy keeps old yards in business and prevents another new one from being built, it would cost shipbuyers perhaps $200 million per year and would not, in fact, result in a larger amount of shipyard capacity, but rather a less efficient set of facilities. (See Section 10-2.)

9-2 Effects of a Work-Dispersion Policy on the Allocation of Orders

Spreading the volume of work in the small program uniformly over all 15 yards requires utilizing about 40 percent of the industry's ways time in Periods I and II, but only 26 percent in Period III. Although no information on the feasibility of various levels of underutilization is available, employment data indicate that at least three yards in the study operated at less than 40 percent utilization of their ways capacity in 1967. Other studies have remarked on the serious underutilization of the industry's capacity.[2] Thus some yards, especially those with related business interests, might survive with substantial idle capacity.

Since presumably it is the maintenance of capital equipment that would motivate a policy of dispersing orders, the requirement on utilization is stated in terms of ways capacity. As a result, the amount of labor relative to ways capacity varies across the yards according to the kinds of ship being built. When inefficient yards are included in the building program, the minimum cost reallocation of ship types calls for them to build ships with relatively small amounts of labor. The main cost differences among yards are labor costs; therefore the cheapest way to maintain a given capital capacity is to use as little labor as possible in high-cost yards. Since merchant ships and tankers tend to have small labor requirements relative to ways time, they would be the orders that are allocated to high-cost yards.

Accordingly, in the small program, the production of 108 small merchant ships, accomplished by two low-cost yards in the original solution, is split among nine yards under a work-dispersion policy. Forty-five large merchant ships are transferred from the two major builders in the earlier solution to three higher-cost yards. Likewise, tanker construction is withdrawn from three efficient firms and awarded instead to three others. The underway replenishment ships and auxiliary ships are moved from the new yard into others. The allocation of destroyers, however, remains relatively undisturbed. They are highly labor-intensive, and the cost of departing from the optimal allocation is greatest for these ships. For less extensive work-dispersal policies, the pattern of transfers is the same but fewer ships are affected. Complications are encountered in applying a work-dispersal policy to yards which are qualified to produce only one or a few ship types, such as submarines or small noncombatant ships, because the numbers of these ships demanded are insufficient to fill the yards' quotas.

With a work-dispersal policy, the pattern (but not the volume) of yard participation in the small program is similar to that of the unconstrained cost-minimizing distribution of the large program. In the latter case, the higher-cost yards receive contracts because the large volume of work fills up the efficient yards. The similarity in distribution of orders indicates that the higher-cost yards have a comparative advantage in building the same ship types, regardless of the reason for which they are accorded the business. The two cases differ significantly, however, in Period III. The work-dispersion policy assures participation of all yards throughout the decade. Otherwise, the high-cost firms would be active in Period III only if demand remained high. The number of ships built by each yard under the three different dispersion policies under the small program are shown in Table 9-2 along with the unconstrained allocation. The beneficiaries of the dispersion policy are easily identified.[3]

A work-dispersion policy reduces the amount of labor-force expansion in the low-cost yards as well as the number of lay-offs at the declining yards. For example, with maximum dispersion under the small program, the increase in skilled employment in the first period is about 3,500 men, some 700 fewer than in the base case. On the other hand, the number of underemployed skilled workers in the industry would drop from about 11,600 to about 9,100, or by 2,500 men. Table 9-3 compares labor-market developments in Period I for the three work-dispersion policies and small demand with the results of the unconstrained allocation.

When demand is high, a policy of dispersing orders becomes redundant during the first two periods since there is adequate work for nearly all yards anyway. Therefore, these policies significantly affect the distribution of contracts for the large building program only in Period III. Table 9-4 compares the allocation of ships with and without dispersion policies for the large program.

9-3 Work-dispersion Policies and Investment in Yard Modernization

Dispersing contracts provides more yards with an incentive to upgrade their machinery and cranes than does the unrestricted allocation. It affects especially

Table 9-2
Numbers of Ships Produced by Yard under Work-dispersion Policies, Small Program

	Maximum Dispersion Period			Medium Dispersion Period			Minimum Dispersion Period			No Dispersion Period		
Shipyard	I	II	III	I	II	III	I	II	III	I	II	III
New Yard	30	31	32	38	41	48	39	39	51	39	42	48
Gulf Coast												
Yard 1	–	8	6	–	15	15	–	18	18	–	19	26
Yard 2	18	18	14	20	19	7	28	26	7	50	54	13
Yard 3	7	8	2	7	8	2	5	5	4	–	–	–
East Coast												
Yard 4	6	7	5	6	5	3	15	7	3	14	13	–
Yard 5	20	18	12	15	14	19	10	10	8	5	–	–
Yard 6	10	11	7	16	9	6	22	22	5	32	32	29
Yard 7	12	12	9	10	10	5	6	6	5	9	–	–
Yard 8	7	8	3	7	8	3	5	5	4	–	–	–
Yard 9	4	4	3	3	3	2	2	2	2	–	–	–
Yard 10	not available			not available			not available			not available		
West Coast												
Yard 11	7	7	5	6	6	3	4	4	3	–	–	–
Yard 12	4	4	4	3	3	2	3	3	2	–	–	–
Yard 13	7	7	5	5	5	3	3	3	3	–	–	–
Yard 14	2	2	1	2	2	1	1	1	1	–	–	–

the less well-equipped yards. As Table 9-5 shows, maximum dispersion of the small program results in equipment-replacement purchases for industry more than twice as great than without dispersion. The West would undertake some investment, but much more occurs in the East. As the minimum utilization requirements are reduced, the investment in the West and East and in total falls sharply, while the Southern component rises slightly.

With the high volume of demand (large program), most yards would be heavily utilized without work-dispersion policies. The total investment of approximately $9 million is affected only minimally by spreading orders. In the high-demand case, all investment occurs in Period I. With the low demand a small amount is carried over to Period II.

The high-cost shipyards with chronic excess capacity find it profitable to purchase new equipment for any contracts they receive. One must not conclude from this, however, that that the dispersion of orders is a good method to induce efficiency in the industry. In final analysis, it remains a subsidy to high-cost yards at the expense of superior competitors and raises the price of ships to buyers.

Table 9-3
Effects of Work-dispersion Policies on Regional Skilled-labor-force Expansion and Contraction, Small Program, Period I

Region: Original Labor Force	Maximum Dispersion	Medium Dispersion	Minimum Dispersion	No Dispersion
South: 12,695				
New hires	1316	2062	2600	3543
Men idle	967	625	511	1224
Difference	349	1437	2089	2319
Net employment change*	833	1750	2345	2931
East: 13,285				
New hires	2213	1409	652	642
Men idle	6052	6461	5564	6186
Difference	−3839	−5052	−4912	−5544
Net employment change	− 813	−1822	−2130	−2451
West: 4,228				
New hires	26	5	0	0
Men idle	2147	2549	3380	4227
Difference	−2121	−2544	−3380	−4227
Net employment change	−1047	−1270	−1690	−2113
12-year Total: 30,208				
New hires	3555	3476	3252	4185
Men idle	9166	9635	9455	11637
Difference	−5611	−6159	−6203	−7452
Net employment change	−1027	−1342	−1475	−1633

*Half of the unemployed workers are assumed to be laid off in each period.

Table 9-4
Numbers of Ships Produced under Work-dispersion Policies, Large Program

	Maximum Dispersion Period			Medium Dispersion Period			Minimum Dispersion Period			No Dispersion Period		
	I	II	III	I	II	III	I	II	III	I	II	III
New Yard	39	41	48	39	41	49	39	40	48	39	41	48
Gulf Coast												
Yard 1	?	17	17	?	23	23	?	22	22	–	22	22
Yard 2	53	43	30	53	55	53	52	53	62	52	52	60
Yard 3	7	8	2	7	8	2	7	6	2	5	3	0
East Coast												
Yard 4	14	14	11	14	18	8	14	19	19	14	17	16
Yard 5	42	33	19	40	27	20	50	34	21	53	53	31
Yard 6	29	28	17	28	29	29	26	29	30	26	28	31
Yard 7	27	24	19	28	23	12	28	23	23	28	28	23
Yard 8	7	8	15	7	8	9	7	6	4	7	–	–
Yard 9	9	8	6	12	6	4	12	3	2	10	7	–
Yard 10	27	23	18	23	18	11	14	7	5	17	–	–
West Coast												
Yard 11	20	13	10	20	10	6	20	20	3	20	20	–
Yard 12	5	10	8	6	8	5	6	16	2	6	16	12
Yard 13	14	12	10	15	10	6	14	4	3	14	–	–
Yard 14	5	4	3	4	3	2	4	2	1	4	–	–

Table 9-5
Value of Equipment Purchases for Existing Yards with and without Work Dispersion, Small Program ($ million)

Extent of Dispersion	Gulf Coast	East Coast	West Coast	Total
Maximum dispersion (40, 40, and 26% util.)				
Undiscounted	$ .98	$2.78	$1.13	$4.89
Discounted (10%)	.91	2.77	1.13	4.81
Medium dispersion (31, 31, and 16% util.)				
Undiscounted	1.05	1.89	.57	3.51
Discounted (10%)	.96	1.89	.57	3.42
Minimum dispersion (19, 19, and 14.5% util.)				
Undiscounted	1.07	1.15	.30	2.52
Discounted (10%)	.95	1.14	.29	2.38
No dispersion				
Undiscounted	1.15	1.15	0	2.30
Discounted (10%)	.98	1.14	0	2.12

10 New Shipyards: Profitability and Prices

It may seem anomalous to consider the possibilities for expansion of capacity in an industry such as shipbuilding whose facilities are now so obviously underutilized. The production-cost differences between a yard like Pascagoula and one of the inefficient older yards are so great, however, that the question of whether to build a new yard is not really a question of expansion but, rather, one of replacement of capacity. Since investment in new shipyards will be a function of returns, the study assesses the expected profitability of the new yard at Pascagoula and attempts to estimate the potential profitability of additional new yards which use the same production techniques.

10-1 Implied Value of Additional New Yards

If the contract price of a ship is set through competitive bidding, then presumably its price will lie near the cost of production in the highest-cost yard in operation. Any yard more efficient than the marginal yard will earn receipts greater than its variable costs. The present value of the differences between expected receipts and variable costs is the value or demand price of the yard. The rate of discount used should be the potential rate of return on alternative investments. Those facilities which produce with the least variable cost will be the ones that have the greatest value.

Any newly built facility will presumably be more efficient and more favorably located than most or all of the existing ones. It will thus tend to displace production from the highest-cost yards, lowering the equilibrium price at which the ships are sold. The demand price for the new yard would be a function of the difference between its production costs and the new equilibrium price level, the latter depending on the level of costs in whichever yard is the marginal one. Which yard in the cost hierarchy ends up being the marginal one depends, in turn, upon the total demand for ships. The higher the demand, the greater the expected difference between price and production costs in an efficient yard.

For a given level of demand, the value of any additional or existing capacity will fall as new yards are constructed. Theoretically, new investment would be carried out to the point where the cost of the last yard built is just equal to or less than its demand price as defined above. Indivisibility of investment and uncertainty about future demand, however, will almost surely prevent the process from being carried out to the point of equality between cost and projected value. The effects of changes in demand on the profitability of new investment was analyzed in the study.

The linear programming model provides a "shadow price" of the ways capacity for each yard. This shadow price might be interpreted as the annual rent that a shipbuilder should be willing to pay for one ways with all complementary facilities which service it, given the number, prices, and kinds of ships the yard is to build. The sum of the rental values over the expected economic life of the facilities, discounted at the prevailing rate of return on capital, provides an estimate of the value of the ways, given the other shipyards in existence and the level of ship demand. A potential demand schedule for new ways capacity can be developed using these present values.

For a given level of ship demand, the effective capacity of the new yard in the model can be increased by discrete amounts. From an analytical point of view, this variation has the same effect as would the inclusion of additional efficient yards. As the number of apparent new yards is increased, the shadow price for additional capacity falls and the value of an additional yard declines. This relationship between the value of an additional new yard and the number already in existence can be plotted graphically and has the same interpretation as a demand schedule for new ways capacity.

The location of such an investment demand schedule depends upon the total projected ship demand. The more ships to be built, the farther right the schedule will shift. As before, two levels of ship demand were postulated in calculating two investment demand schedules. In both cases it was assumed that new yard capacity could be provided in increments equal to half that of the Pascagoula yard. To locate the investment schedule under the small program, it was unnecessary to evaluate new yard capacity at more than two points. These two points assumed additional new capacity equal to 50 and 100 percent that of the Pascagoula yard.

The large program shifted the investment schedule markedly, and evaluation of new yards was done under assumptions of capacity additions equal to 50, 100, 150, and 200 percent that of Pascagoula. The implicit rental values obtained at these points were discounted at 10 percent to obtain the demand prices. Using this rate of return, the influence of rents beyond the decade on present value is negligible. Figure 10-1 shows the two investment-demand curves derived from the analysis. The horizontal line is a supply curve which assumes that a yard such as Pascagoula can be reproduced for an investment of $135 million.

The present value of the new Litton yard is given by the vertical intercept of both schedules. Under the small program, it is somewhat greater than the estimated cost, implying a compounded rate of return of slightly over 10 percent per annum. The value of additional capacity quickly falls below the cost, however. One would predict, therefore, that if this amount of demand was

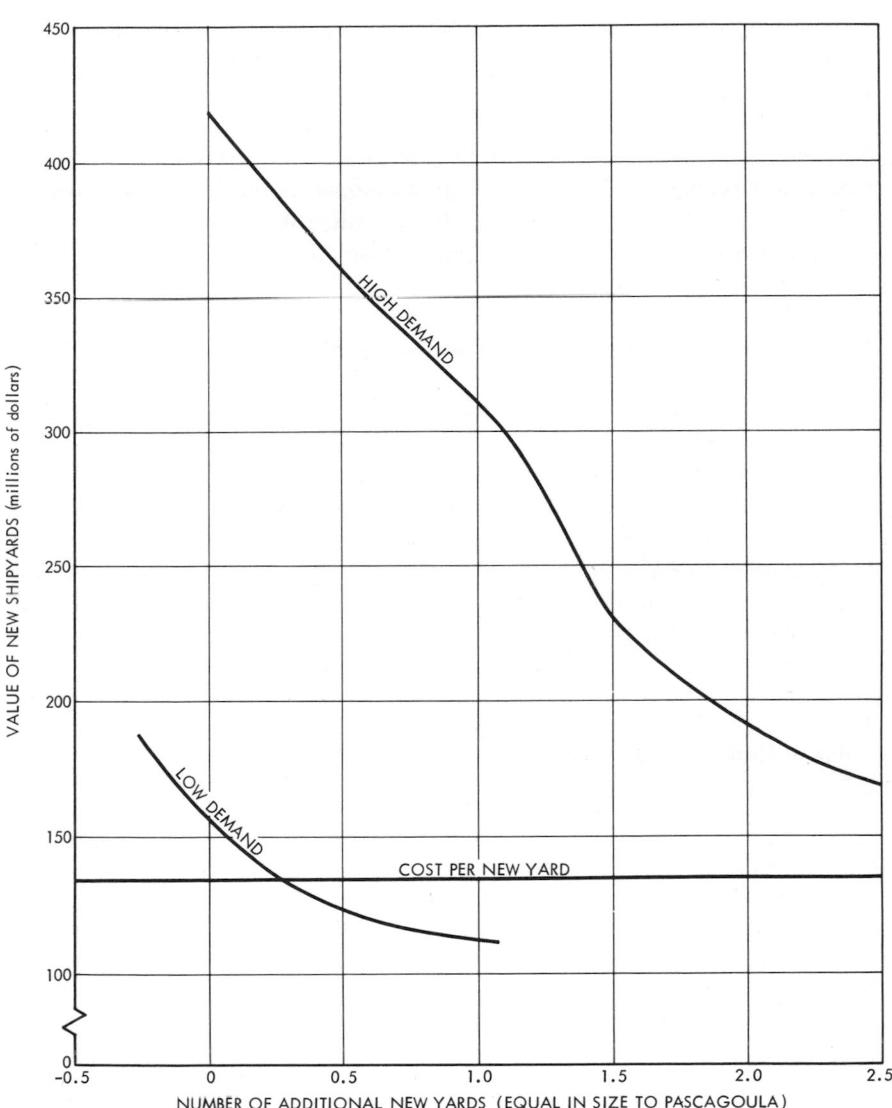

Figure 10–1. Value of new-yard capacity.

projected, no more new yards would be forthcoming. On the other hand, at the high demand level, two or more additional new yards could profitably be added to the industry at a cost of $135 million per yard. The data from which the two schedules are derived are given in more detail in Table 10-1.

If the new yards were to be built under the large program, they would compete directly with the less efficient of the yards now in existence. As these yards lost business, they would have less incentive to modernize their own facilities. Figure 10-2 indicates how aggregate investment in modernization by old yards would decline as capacity in new yards is increased. Gulf Coast yards would be virtually unaffected. East Coast equipment purchases would decline continuously with expansion of new capacity while West Coast yards would be affected only after a second new yard equal in site to Litton had been built.

10-2 Effects on Ship Prices of Increased New-yard Capacity

In Chapter 5, we discussed the technique of using shadow prices for estimating the probable bid prices for various ships. These estimates were obtained for the two different levels of demand and were based upon the configuration and capacity of the industry as it exists now, including the Litton yard at Pascagoula. If additional new yards were to be built, their efficiency should be reflected in a fall in ship prices at each demand level. A comparison between the original estimates and those projected if more new yards were to be built is provided in Tables 10-2 and 10-3.

Table 10-1
Value of Modern Yard ($ millions)

	Normal Capacity	50% Increase	100% Increase	150% Increase	200% Increase
Low Demand					
Annual rent value–1st 4 years	16.126	9.922	13.001		
Annual rent value–2nd 4 years	22.481	18.812	17.953	(not tested)	
Annual rent value–3rd 4 years	15.561	15.472	7.452		
Total value for 12 years (discount rate = 10%)	155.292	120.256	115.168		
High Demand					
Annual rent value–1st 4 years	64.321	55.646	46.003	31.942	25.090
Annual rent value–2nd 4 years	39.924	35.390	32.166	23.794	23.012
Annual rent value–3rd 4 years	28.690	22.775	21.955	18.313	17.339
Total value for 12 years (discount rate = 10%)	420.492	362.276	313.328	227.312	195.936
Expected cost: $135 million					

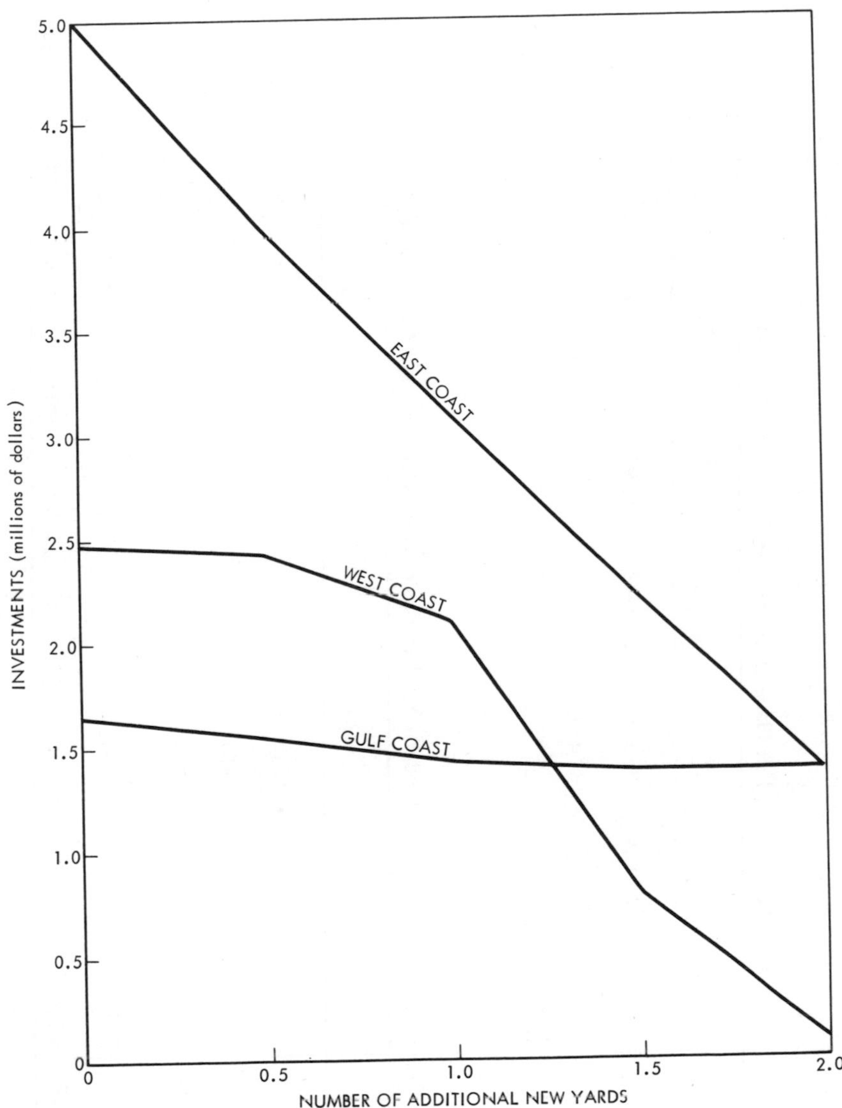

Figure 10–2. Regional investments in yard modernization as a function of new yard construction (high-demand).

Table 10-2
Cost Reduction Due to Second Modern Yard in Place (Low Demand, 1969 $ Millions)

	Ship								
	1	2	3	4	5	6	7	8	9
Marginal cost (original cap.)	58.2875	22.4413	33.1212	19.6863	13.9482	37.5489	17.7430	42.0837	7.7403
Marginal cost (one added yard)	57.0378	21.6102	32.4595	18.8713	13.4904	36.1418	17.0171	40.5108	7.4640
Saving	1.2497	0.8311	0.6617	0.8150	0.4578	1.4071	0.7259	1.5729	0.2763

Table 10-3
Cost Reduction Due to Second and Third Modern Yard in Place (High Demand, 1969 $ Millions)

	Ship									
	1	2	3	4	5	6	7	8	9	10
Marginal cost (original cap.)	64.4808	26.6741	37.6219	21.2048	16.3760	41.7307	21.6263	46.3109	9.8856	27.5136
Marginal cost (one added yard)	62.1591	25.0109	36.0489	20.2842	15.8292	40.0586	20.1332	44.6531	9.1233	25.9137
Marginal cost (two added yards)	59.1145	22.9320	33.8313	19.9673	14.3420	37.7496	18.2315	42.1846	8.1267	23.8497
Saving (one added yard)	2.3217	1.6632	1.5730	.9206	.5468	1.6721	1.4931	1.6578	.7623	1.5999
Saving (two added yards)	5.3663	3.7421	3.7906	1.2375	2.0340	3.9811	3.3948	4.1263	1.7589	3.6639

Under the large program, building an additional new yard should reduce prices by 3 to 8 percent. On the average, these savings would amount to around $90 million per year, reducing the average annual budget to about $1.6 billion. If two additional yards were constructed, savings per ship would range from 7 to 17 percent, or perhaps $200 million per year. Under the small program, an additional new yard is not likely to be profitable. If, nevertheless, it were built, prices would fall from 2 to 4 percent, and budget savings would be about $25 million annually.

It is possible that a general expectation of sustained high demand would induce the construction of additional new shipyards designed for series production. It is frequently alleged, however, that, in addition to high demand, a policy of contracting for large numbers of ships at one time is a necessary incentive to the yards to build. If this proposition is true, then the savings listed above provide for the U.S. taxpayer an approximation of the value of a policy of awarding contracts extending for a number of years, rather than making smaller awards periodically during the decade. In the same vein, it was suggested in Chapter 9 that the loss of these savings is one component of the cost to the taxpayer of conducting a work-dispersion policy in shipbuilding.

11 Summary and Conclusions

This study has examined the effects of alternative shipbuilding programs and government procurement policies on the size and location of the U.S. private shipbuilding industry and on the cost of ships projected until 1980. The results were obtained using a linear programming model that simulates the activities of 15 private shipyards. The model matches different levels of demands for ships against existing and potential shipbuilding capacity. For the purposes of examining resource allocation, it was assumed that the firms set their prices without collusion and are obliged through sealed bidding to price near marginal cost for each job.

The model minimizes the construction costs of ships to be built between 1969 and 1980 using 15 shipyards. Ship types were combined into 10 categories that are composites of specific designs. For instance, destroyers with and without guided-missile systems were combined; cargo liners were combined with container ships.

As inputs to the analytical model, estimates were made of the variable costs of building the ships in each qualified yard with facilities and manpower as of 1969. These estimates were differentiated by yard in accordance with each yard's equipment and by regional wage levels. Progress functions ("learning curves") were used in the calculation of costs and labor requirements for multi-ship runs. Constraints were imposed as a function of potential resource utilization rates and existing capacity. The costs of increasing the rate of ship construction by adding labor and the costs and benefits of investment in improved equipment were also incorporated into the model.

In the program solution, ship orders were allocated first to yards with the lowest production costs. As these yards expand production, their costs rise, or their capacity is reached and other, less efficient yards begin receiving orders. Ship types were distributed among participating yards on the basis of production costs. The model was used to test the implications of two alternative volumes of shipbuilding, encompassing naval and commercial ships. The smaller program (36 ships per year) was based on a projection made in 1969, while the larger program (about 70 per year) included much higher rates of both commercial and naval construction. Different delivery schedules were tested for each program.

11-1 Shipbuilding Activity, Employment, and Capacity Utilization

The cost-minimizing strategy chosen by the linear program led to results which are unexpected and provocative. For the smaller program, for instance, the model consolidated orders into eight shipyards, excluding from large ship construction several recent and current participants. Only the five most efficient yards—three of them in the South—would receive orders after the mid-1970s. Other yards would be obliged to turn to the construction of smaller ships, or to repair and conversions, or fold. Moreover, no ships would be built on the West Coast. This distribution of shipbuilding activity is a consequence of regional wage differences and of disparities in productive efficiency.

The larger shipbuilding program would sustain 9 or 10 yards, including one in the West, in good economic health throughout the decade. Five yards would utilize their capacity fully. Even with this relatively high demand, however, a cost-minimizing distribution of orders would leave five or six firms without work in the late 1970s. Such heavy demand would probably impel the construction of new yards, further undercutting existing yards and altering the location of the industry.

The pattern of employment fluctuations closely parallels the rate of shipbuilding activity. For the nation as a whole, the cost-minimizing distribution of the smaller demand program would result in substantial contraction of shipyard employment. Skilled employment would shrink by at least 12,000 workers over the 12-year period. Absorption of these skilled laborers into other industries such as construction or aerospace would depend on the general level of economic activity. Generalization, however, obscures certain regional labor-market developments, such as substantial new hiring in the early 1970s in several Eastern and Southern yards followed by a return to initial levels.

Under the large shipbuilding program, a rapid expansion of the labor force takes place in many shipyards, although the industry as a whole shows a net expansion of only 2,000 skilled men for the decade. Only the South would employ more men in 1980 than in 1967. The East Coast yards would expand sharply in the early 1970s but return to slightly under their original employment by 1980. The West Coast yards would end the decade with only 40 percent of their initial labor force. Full freedom on the part of yards to reschedule production in order to eliminate peaks and slumps would reduce the need to hire labor that later must be laid off. While this change would result in a more stable labor force, it would yield only negligible savings in shipbuilding costs.

11-2 Investments in Shipyard Modernization

The magnitude of investment—both replacement of present equipment and construction of entire new yards—depends largely on the level of demand and the vintage of equipment in present yards.

Heavy demand would elicit more investment in modernization of existing yards by bringing into use less efficient capacity with its greater need for renovation. According to the model, under the small ship program, two existing yards in the East and two in the South would undertake thorough modernization of their equipment. With the large program, two additional Eastern yards would invest to the limit. The Western yards, on the other hand, would fall further behind in productive efficiency, because even the large program is insufficient to stimulate a full modernization in more than one yard. Barring a boom in repairs for the Pacific tanker fleet, only a costly government policy of deliberate dispersion of order would impel further upgrading of Western facilities.

Even if these investments were made to upgrade existing yards, the erection of new yards appears to be profitable. With the small shipbuilding program, our analysis indicates that the cost of the new yard in Mississippi could be recouped with a 10 percent return in 12 years. With a large demand for ships, the cost of two additional new yards of this size could be fully recouped. The construction of these new yards, of course, would preclude some of the replacement investments in existing yards discussed above.

11-3 Ship Prices and Production Costs[1]

The prices of ships to buyers are higher than the variable production costs of all but the marginal yard in the program. Prices vary with the volume of demand. The minimized variable shipyard cost for the small shipbuilding program should average about $830 million per year at 1968 prices. The price to the buyers is estimated to be about $875 million, or only 5 percent higher. This difference would constitute the return to invested capital and risk. It is a greater percentage for lower-cost yards and near zero for those high-cost yards receiving orders. Prices of various ships fall by 5 to 10 percent as production rates taper off during the decade. With the large program, the minimized shipyard cost should average about $1.5 billion per year, while the buyers' price in this case, at $1.7 billion, is about 13 percent higher. The greater difference reflects that, at least during the peak production years, yards are selling at prices which are higher by 8 to 29 percent than in the small program.

Construction of additional new yards would supplant certain less efficient yards in satisfying the demand and would generate lower costs and prices. If a second new yard were constructed, as indicated for the large program, ship prices would fall by between 3 and 8 percent.

If an average price decline of 5 percent per ship is assumed, buyers would save roughly $90 million per year. The construction of a third new yard would reduce the buyers' bill by at least again as much. Given the cost of new yards, these calculations appear to make the entry of new yards of clear benefit to the taxpayer, even if the yards must be government-financed.

11-4 The Impact of Work-dispersion Policies

Because of the geographical changes in the production locations implied in cost-minimizing procurement, the costs and other implications of deliberate dispersal of government contracts were examined. A policy of equalizing capacity utilization in all yards under the small program would yield uniform use rates of 40 percent through the mid-1970s and only 26 percent thereafter. The extra cost of this program to the buyers would be about $80 million per year. Nine yards would benefit at the expense of four others. The cost of maintaining the inefficient yards at lower utilization rates would be somewhat less. The larger the total demand, the less relevant and costly dispersion policies become, although more yards are penalized to sustain the few being subsidized. Naturally, a policy of spreading the work reduces the amount of labor-force expansion in the low-cost yards of the South and East and cuts idleness and lay-offs in the high-cost yards.

Despite the fact that dispersion of orders would boost the rate of equipment replacement in existing yards, it is not a method of promoting industry efficiency but remains a subsidy to high-cost yards. Indeed, if dispersion policies result in excess capacity in the new yard, they are likely to render this yard unprofitable and are certain to discourage the erection of additional new yards.

Appendixes

Appendix A
A Linear Programming Model of the U.S. Shipbuilding Industry

The results described in this report were derived using a linear programming model that simulates the production activities of the shipbuilding industry in the United States. Certain components of the model are discussed more fully in other appendixes. Here we deal with the model as a whole in an attempt to provide a comprehensive picture of the shipbuilding allocation process as it is conceived in the report.

A-1 Linear Programming

Problems that involve the maximization or minimization of a numerical function in which the variables are subject to constraints form a general class called optimization problems. An important subclass of these are linear programming problems. The mathematical definition of linear programming is a simple one. It is the analysis of problems in which a linear function of a number of variables is to be maximized (or minimized) when these variables are subject to a number of linear inequalities.

Linear programming deals with special types of the general economic problem of allocating scarce resources to achieve given objectives. There may be many feasible ways in which the resources can be combined but very few of them are likely to be *efficient*. We define efficiency as a state in which output of no single product can be increased without decreasing the output of one or more other products. Once it is known which combinations of resources are efficient, it still is necessary to choose from among them the combination that best fulfills a particular objective.

The resources may be one or more of a variety of inputs such as land, labor, machine time, or money. The objective may be to maximize production of one or several goods, to minimize the cost of producing these same goods, to maximize the net return from production, or to maximize gross return on investment in financial assets. Whatever the goal, it is defined in terms of *activities*. If the objective is to maximize production of several goods or to minimize the cost of producing these same goods, the production of each good is an activity. The variables we spoke of earlier are the levels at which each of the activities are operated. If the problem is one of production, the variable for each activity is the number of each of the goods produced. A *program* is a list of the levels chosen for each activity.

The activity levels have significance only if the objective is defined. Otherwise, variables associated with each activity are just so much algebra. We must have *criteria* by which to judge the merits of different programs. If the goal is to minimize costs, the criteria are the costs associated with producing a unit of each good. If the goal is maximization of gross return, the criteria are the returns associated with sale of a unit of each good.

When we combine the criteria and the activity levels defined by a particular program, we obtain a "figure of merit" for that program. Thus, if c_1 and c_2 are criterion values, per unit, for each of two products and x_1 and x_2 are activity levels for these products given by a particular program, then $z = c_1x_1 + c_2x_2$ is the figure of merit for that program. We shall call $c_1x_2 + c_2x_2$ the "criterion function," the "objective function," or simply the "functional."

Operation of each of the activities at a certain level requires the use of resources. It was postulated earlier that these resources were limited. The levels at which the various activities can be carried on thus depends on how much of each resource the activity requires and the total amount of each resource available. The ratio between a unit of production in one activity and the amount of a resource required for that unit of production is called a *production coefficient* or, more generally, a *structural coefficient* of the problem.

A is a matrix of structural coefficients, and b is a vector of stipulation values for the amounts of resources available; c' is a vector of criteria, either prices, costs, or rates of return. A, b, and c' are parameters of the problem. Only the vector of activity levels x can be varied to affect the solution of the problem. The decision maker is interested in choosing a program, an x vector, that optimizes his criterion function.[1]

Solution of a linear programming problem can yield much more information than just the optimal value of the criterion function and the level at which all activities should be operated in order to achieve this value. The data from which the original linear programming problem was formed (which we shall call the "direct" or "primal" problem) can also be used to form another problem called the "dual." If the primal problem is a maximization problem, the dual is a minimization problem, and vice versa. The solution value for the criterion functions is the same for both.

We can show the relationship between the primal and the dual problems by laying out the structure of a simple two-variable, two-constraint problem.

		Primal variables (maximize)		Primal stipulations = dual criteria	
		x_1	x_2		
Dual variables	w_1	a_{11}	a_{12}	$\leqslant$	b_1
(minimize)	w_2	a_{21}	a_{22}	$\geqslant$	b_2
		$\leqslant$	$\leqslant$		
Primal criteria= dual stipulations		c_1	c_2		

The primal problem is:

1. Maximize: $c_1x_1 + c_2x_2$

The sum of the products of the structural coefficients with the levels of each activity gives the total amount of that resource needed for a particular program. The amount needed cannot exceed the total amount on hand, although it may be less than the total available, the remainder being unused excess. If a_{ij} is the structural coefficient defining the relationship between activity j and resource i, and b_i is the total amount of resource i available, then the constraint imposed upon the use of resource i can be written as $\sum_j a_{ij}x_j \leqslant b_i$.

If there were only two activities and two resources, the constraints would be

$$a_{11}x_1 + a_{12}x_2 \leqslant b_1$$

$$a_{12}x_1 + a_{12}x_2 \leqslant b_2$$

The b_i's are *stipulations*. They are the limiting values on each of the available resources. An additional constraint is that the activities cannot be operated at a negative level. Thus,

$$x_j \geqslant 0 \quad j = 1, \ldots, n$$

A complete statement of the linear programming problem with two activities and two constraints is:

Maximize: $c_1x_1 + c_2x_2$

Subject to: $a_{11}x_1 + a_{12}x_2 \leqslant b_1$

$a_{21}x_1 + a_{22}x_2 \leqslant b_2$

$x_1{}'x_2 \geqslant 0$

The general problem is:

Maximize: $\sum_j c_jx_j$

Subject to: $\sum_j a_{ij}x_j \leqslant b_i' \quad i = 1, \ldots, n$

$x_i \geqslant 0$

or:

Maximize: $c'x$

Subject to: $Ax \leqslant b$

$x \geqslant 0$

Subject to:

$$a_{11}x_1 + a_{12}x_2 \leqslant b_1$$
$$a_{21}x_1 + a_{22}x_2 \leqslant b_2$$
$$x_1 'x_2 \geqslant 0$$

The dual problem is:

Minimize:

$$b_1 w_1 + b_2 w_2$$

Subject to:

$$a_{11} w_1 + a_{21} w_2 \geqslant c_1$$
$$a_{21} w_1 + a_{22} w_2 \geqslant c_2$$
$$w_1 'w_2 \geqslant 0$$

The question arises as to what kinds of activities are represented by the dual variables, the *w*'s. The word activity is somewhat misleading in this context. When we were talking about production of goods in the primal problem, activity seemed to be quite suitable nomenclature, and the activity levels were measured in terms of units of production.[2] The dual variables, however, are not units but prices.[3] The dual activities can thus be thought of as pricing activities. The objective in minimizing the dual functional, $b_1 w_1 + b_2 w_2$, is to choose a set of prices for the inputs b_1 and b_2 that minimizes their total value, subject to the constraint that the cost of inputs for a unit of production of each good is greater than or equal to the price of the good. When an optimal solution is arrived at, the only constraints operative are satisfied as equalities, and these constraints are associated with the goods produced. Any good associated with a constraint in which the costs of production are greater than the price will not be produced. The value of the primal variable for that activity will be zero.

There is a dual variable associated with each of the constraints from the primal problem. The stipulation values, the b_i's, for these primal constraints become the criteria for the objective function of the dual. Once an optimum solution is reached for either the primal or the dual problem, the dual variables give the value to the program of a unit change in each of the primal stipulation values. In other words, the values assigned the dual variables by an optimal program are the marginal values of a unit of each imput. They are usually called "shadow prices," "dual evaluators," or "dual prices."

The dual prices are internal to the problem. They are derived from the value of the output. Their importance lies in the fact that once they are known, it is possible to evaluate the profitability of changing the constraint stipulations. It may be possible to trade advantageously some of one input whose dual price is very low or zero for more of an input whose dual price is very high. The dual evaluators are valid only over a definite range of stipulation values that depends upon the problem.

There is another interesting and important property of the dual variables. Whenever one of the constraints of the primal problem is redundant, i.e., there is more of the input than needed, the dual price for that constraint will be zero.[4] Conversely, the activity level of the primal will be zero whenever the sum of costs (as measured by the dual prices) for inputs to that activity exceeds the return associated with it. Stated mathematically:

$$w_i = 0 \quad \text{whenever } \sum_j x_j a_{ij} < b_i$$

$$x_j = 0 \quad \text{whenever } \sum_j w_i a_{ij} > c_j$$

The first condition merely means that the marginal value of an input that is already in excess supply is zero. The second condition means that no activity will be undertaken whose cost of production exceeds its return.

It is not necessary to solve both the primal and the dual problems in order to obtain values for both the primal and dual variables. Solution of one or the other problem yields both sets of values. In addition, there are techniques of parametric programming that make it possible to determine the ranges of stipulation values over which the dual prices are valid as measures of marginal values of inputs, and the ranges over which the criteria associated with activities can be varied without changing the optimal program. All this information is readily available as output if the problem is one that can be solved by a standard computer program.

We now have enough information about the general linear programming problem and the properties of its solution to proceed to the specific problem of the allocation of ship demand to shipyards.

A-2 The Shipbuilding Industry

The behavior of the shipbuilding industry, in which prices are determined in competitive bidding, is sufficiently similar to the model of pure competition that the usual competitive assumptions concerning investment and long- and short-run cost curves for the firm apply.[5] Although the model is a linear one, it has been designed to take account of the increasing cost portion of the short-run cost curve and also to accommodate the effects of increased productivity and cost saving resulting from investment in new plant and equipment.

The objective of the program is to minimize the total variable cost of producing any given set of fleet requirements. It is assumed that pricing for bids would reflect costs of production for various yards and, therefore, that an allocation of ships on the basis of overall cost minimization in the model should reflect, with a fair degree of accuracy, the results to be expected from a competitive bidding process.

A-3 Object Function

The objective function, whose value is to be minimized in solving the problem is:

$$\sum_{n}\sum_{i}\sum_{j}\sum_{k}\Big(C_{ijk}X_{ijk} + F_{njk}Y_{njk} + F'_{njk}Y'_{njk} + F''_{njk}Y''_{njk} + \theta N_{jk} + R_{jk}I_{jk} + R'_{jk}I'_{jk} + R''_{jk}I''_{jk} + P_{ijk}V_{ijk} - S_{ijk}Z_{ijk}\Big)$$

There are *i* ship types, *j* shipyards, and *k* time periods for which these costs must be summed. The *n* subscript refers to the number of labor activities. $C_{ijk}X_{ijk}$ is the cost of producing ships using production processes and yard facilities currently in existence. If there were no possibilities for expansion of labor supply or investment in new equipment or adopting large shipways to build smaller ships, this would be the only component of the objective function. However, provision is made for doing all these things.

Labor Expansion

The three $F_{njk}Y_{njk}$ activities serve two closely related functions. First, they permit the existing supply of each of *n* types of labor to be expanded beyond the amount initially given for each firm. Thus, if the stock of one or more types of labor is exhausted, the firm can supplement this stock by hiring more people (which may also involve training the unskilled) and by working overtime or adding more shifts.

Second, these activities provide a means of approximating the rising portion of the cost curve. As output is expanded beyond the minimum cost point by increasing the work force, unit costs can be expected to rise. They rise initially because with a fixed capital stock, the ratio of inputs changes from the optimal and, if there is an upward-sloping supply curve for labor, the labor costs will increase. Both these effects can be taken into account and approximated by using a succession of three labor-expansion activities.

Labor Attrition

Each yard begins each period with a given labor supply. If the yard does not utilize all the labor it has available, at least part of the excess presumably will be lost to it in the future, reducing its future labor pool. The N_{jk} activities are essentially slack variables that take on the value of the unused labor in each yard. Since there is no out-of-pocket cost associated with not using the labor, the coefficient ϕ is equal to zero. There is a cost to the yard only if it must replace part of this labor later through the Y (labor expansion) activities. The release of surplus labor is represented through the role of this activity in the labor constraint (see Section A-2).

Investment

The next three elements $R_{jk}I_{jk}$, $R'_{jk}I'_{jk}$, and $R''_{jk}I''_{jk}$ are investment activities that permit improvements in drafting, steel cutting, and crane capacity, respectively. The unit of measure is \$100,000 worth of investment. Investment has two effects on the production function. It lowers the cost of building each ship, and it makes possible more efficient utilization of labor and ways in the resource constraints (Section A-2). The lower cost is, of course, a reflection of the greater efficiency, but each of these effects appears separately in the program.

The investment variables represent three distinct types of investment which have different rates of return and different effects on the utilization of labor. The first two activities involve investment in equipment that affects the productivity of only the hull labor. These two are separated into a high- and low-return activity. The third activity, which is investment in crane capacity, must be distinguished from the other two because it affects the productivity of outfitting as well as hull labor. The activities specifically exclude expansion of ways and docks capacity.

The R_{jk}, R'_{jk}, and R''_{jk} elements are coefficients that convert a lump sum of investment of \$100,000 into an equivalent rental fee for a time span less than the life of the equipment. The time span varies among time periods in the model and measures the number of years remaining in the model over which the equipment could be used. For example, in the final period, the rental fee would cover only four years.[6]

Ways Substitution

It is assumed that each ship will be built on the smallest ways that will accommodate it in each yard. However, if a yard does not have the appropriate-size ways or if it has no available capacity left of the correct size, it can build smaller ships on larger ways. Using larger ways than necessary involves the opportunity cost of wasted building space. Therefore the $P_{ijk}V_{ijk}$ activities permit the substitution to take place and assign a cost to it which is only large enough to prevent its being done unnecessarily.

Cost Reduction

The final element in the objective function is what might be termed a cost reduction activity, S_kZ_{jk}. The S_k is fixed for each yard in a single time period but varies across periods as a function of the rate of discount. The Z_{jk} represents the number of units of \$100,000 savings that the yard is able to realize when building ships. The values that Z_{jk} can reach depend on the amount of new equipment that is purchased with the investment activity.

A-4 Constraints

Labor-utilization Constraints

The first three constraints are on the utilization of three mutally exclusive types of skilled labor: outfitting, electronic, and hull-construction labor. Each type of ship requires a certain amount of each class of labor. Since each yard differs somewhat from the others in its production process, the amount of labor required per ship also varies by yard. The initial amounts of hull, electronic and outfitting labor are H_{jk} , F_{jk}, and O_{jk}, respectively.

The constraint on hull labor is written:

$$\sum_{i=1}^{10} a_{hijk}X_{ijk} - Y_{hjk} - Y'_{hjk} - Y''_{hjk} - e_{hjk}I_{jk} - e'_{hjk}I'_{jk}$$

$$- e''_{hjk}I''_{jk} + 1/2\, N_{hjk-1} + N_{hjk} = H_{jk} \quad \text{for } k\text{-}1,3; j=1,15$$

The a_{hijk} is the hull labor required per ship type i in yard j in time period k. These requirements are summed for all 10 ship categories in the model. Y_{hjk} is the amount of hull labor added with the initial labor-expansion activity. Y'_h and Y''_h are the higher-cost labor-expansion activities. Making the Y's negative on the left-hand side of the equation has the same effect as adding them to the pool on the right-hand side. The $e_{hjk}I_{jk}$, $e'_{hjk}I'_{jk}$, and $e''_{hjk}I''_{jk}$ are the hull-labor savings available from the investment activities. If investment is undertaken, the amount of labor required per ship is reduced. The reduction has the same effect as would an increase in the total supply, as far as the constraint is concerned.

The N_{hjk} is the slack variable that represents the unused hull-labor pool and makes the constraint an equation instead of an inequality. One-half N_{hjk-1} is one-half the previous period's unemployed labor. It is assumed that these people have found jobs elsewhere or dropped out of the labor force, thereby reducing the available pool of labor.

The other two labor constraints are written somewhat differently. The hull labor is the only type of labor affected by all three of the investment activities.

The electronic labor is not affected by any of them and therefore is written much more simply as

$$\sum_{i=1}^{10} a_{eijk}X_{ijk} - Y_{ejk} - Y'_{ejk} - Y''_{ejk} + 1/2N_{ejk-1} + N_{ejk} = E_{jk}$$

for $k = 1,3; j = 1,15$

The third constraint is that on the outfitting labor. The productivity of outfitting labor is affected by investment in crane capacity and so the constraint is

$$\sum_{i=1}^{10} a_{oijk}X_{ijk} - Y_{ojk} - Y'_{ojk} - Y''_{ojk} - e''_{ojk}I''_{jk} + 1/2N_{ojk-1} + N_{ojk} = O_{jk}$$

for $k = 1, 3; j = 1, 15$

Labor-training Constraints

The next two constraints are those on the amount of labor that can be added to the labor force at a given cost per man-hour. The labor-supply curve presumably slopes upward, and the program simulates the upward slope by constraining the amounts that can be acquired at lower costs. The constraints are written:

$$Y_{njk} \leqslant B_{njk} \qquad \text{for all } n, j, k$$

$$Y'_{njk} \leqslant B'_{njk} \qquad \text{all } n, j, k$$

There is no constraint on Y''_{njk}. The B's are set as a uniform fraction of each yard's initial labor force.

Ways Constraint

The next set of constraints is imposed by the number of building positions in each yard. The units in which ways capacity is measured are the total number of years available on these facilities. Since each time period in the model covers four years, the stipulation value of the constraint for each yard is four ways years for each shipways or drydock in existence. Each building position falls into one of three size groups, and there is a constraint on the yard for each size of ways that it has. Each ship is allocated to the minimum-size ways upon which it can be built. If there is no ways space of the optimal size available, the yard incurs a penalty in building the ship on a larger size ways. The constraint for the smallest ways size is written:

$$\sum_{i=1}^{10} p_{ijk}X_{ijk} - V_{ljk} - m_{jk}Y_{jk}\, m'_{jk}\, Y'_{jk} - m''_{jk}Y''_{jk} - g_{jk}I_{jk} - g'_{jk}I'_{jk} - g''_{jk}I''_{jk} \leqslant W_{sjk}$$

The p_{ijk} is the number of ways years required for construction of a ship of type i and, of course, varies among ships as well as among yards for a given ship type. The $-V_{ljk}$ is the additional ways time that can be used on larger ways if the small-ways capacity is fully utilized. W_{sjk} is the ways time available.

The total ways capacity cannot be increased directly in the program since there is no expansion or investment function that affects the size or number of ways. However, both the labor expansion and investment activities have indirect effects on the ways constraint because they reduce the necessary ways time required per ship. Expansion of the labor force reduces the necessary ways time because it includes increased shift and overtime work, which means that less calendar time is required to complete a ship. The investment activities affect a ways constraint to the extent that purchased equipment not only saves on labor but reduces the amount of time required to complete a given task on the shipways. Investments may also have the purpose of reorganizing production to transfer work from the ways to other areas. Thus, both these time savings have the net effect of increasing ways capacity.

Demand

The demand-requirements constraint is written as

$$\sum_{j=1}^{15} \sum_{k=1}^{t} X_{ijk} \geqslant D_{it} \qquad \text{for each of 10 ship types}$$

The number of ships of each type required for the fleet at the end of any point in time, D_{it}, may be supplied from production in previous periods. The model can thus allocate construction intertemporally as well as among shipyards.

Investment

Another set of constraints specifies the amount of each type of investment that the yard can undertake before it reaches its capacity to absorb the new equipment. Some yards already have the equipment that is included in other yards' potential investment. The more modern yards will have only one or two investment activities and constraints, because other investments would be redundant for them. The constraint on each investment function is typically written

$$\sum_{k=1}^{3} I_{jk} \leqslant P_j$$

Efficient Production Capacity

This constraint specifies the limit imposed on production of ships with the newly purchased, more efficient equipment. The greater the amount of investment, the larger the number of ships that can be built at the lower cost. The constraint, as written for period t, is

$$\sum_{k=1}^{t} h_{jk}I_{jk} + \sum_{k=1}^{t} h'_{jk}I'_{jk} - \sum_{i=1}^{15} l_iZ_{ijk} \geqslant 0 \quad \text{for all } j \text{ and } k$$

Each unit of investment, I_{jk}, provides the yard with facilities to build more efficiently h_{jk} standard ships per time period where one of the ship types is arbitrarily designated as the standard ship. Since the second part of the investment function provides lower returns, h'_{jk} is less than h_{jk}.

This capacity is absorbed by the construction of ships in that yard. Because the absorption rate varies by ship, the coefficient l_i is the ratio between the standard ship and ship i. Thus, building a larger ship absorbs more of the efficient capacity than building a smaller one. All investment undertaken prior to and during the period in which the ship is built adds to efficient capacity for that period.

Cost-reduction Limit

The final equation has been labeled cost-reduction limit primarily for lack of a better name. Because the coefficient of the cost-reduction activity in the objective function is negative, the program will undertake as much as permitted of this activity in minimizing the function. It does not recognize the logical connection between activities Z (saving) and X (building ships). The solution must therefore be prevented from claiming economies on ships which were never demanded or built. The necessary constraint is written

$$\sum_{i=1}^{10} x_{ijk} - \sum_{i=1}^{15} z_{ijk} \geqslant 0 \qquad \text{all, } j, k, \text{ and } i$$

Appendix B
Costs, Labor Use, and Ways Requirements Data

This appendix describes the way in which the standard first-ship costs and resource-utilization rates were derived. These steps precede the differentiation of these data by yard and their conversion to average coefficients for production runs in the model.[1]

Government planning estimates of costs, manhour inputs, and ways use for naval and commercial ships served as the starting point for calculating the coefficients used in the model. The preliminary steps in processing these data were to break down the estimates into its subcomponents and to convert each estimate to a first-ship basis.

B-1 Subdivision of Costs and Labor Hours

Costs were divided into separate components attributable to (1) shipboard equipment which is supplied by the government but installed by the shipyard,[2] (2) materials (e.g., steel and paint) purchased by the yards, (3) directly allocable shipyard labor costs, and (4) shipyard overhead. This division was done using proportions derived from data on U.S. programs between 1958 and 1965. The average historical proportions for all ship contracts in each generic ship category (surface combatants, submarines, tankers, etc.) were used to allocate costs for future ships of that category.[3]

The proportion of government-furnished equipment differs mainly between combatant ships, for which it is typically one-third to one-half of total cost, and noncombatant ships for which it commonly runs from one-sixth to one-fourth. After this component was removed, the proportions of the remaining cost categories averaged about the same for all generic ship types. Of this remainder, an average of 27 percent went for shipyard labor, about 55 percent for materials, and some 18 percent for overhead.

The cost of government-furnished equipment was eliminated from further consideration. Shipyard labor and materials costs together comprise the variable cost of ship construction but were dealt with separately because of the differing rates of cost progress ("learning") applicable to each of them. It is these variable costs which specify the model's objective function. Shipyard overhead costs were ignored except when figuring total costs to the buyers of a shipbuilding program. All costs were standardized in 1968 prices, using separate indices for labor and materials costs.[4]

Although labor costs were handled as an aggregate, data for the model's constraints on the use of direct labor hours in shipbuilding were divided along functional lines among those devoted to (1) hull construction, (2) electrical installations, and (3) nonelectrical installations and outfitting. Separate constraints on the use of these types of labor were applied to each shipyard, permitting the model to take some cognizance of the composition as well as the total amount of labor required. Shipyards estimate direct labor inputs in these categories in their documentation of bids, and the average proportions for bids tendered between 1958 and 1965 in each generic ship category were used to break down estimated labor requirements for future ships. Unofficial estimates of the proportions were used for the merchant ships. Table B-1 shows the proportions applied to each category. Shipyard drafting and lofting, although retained in the cost data, were eliminated from labor hours, because it was not practicable to include this type of manpower in the constraints.

B-2 Calculation of First-ship Cost and Labor Hours

The data provided by the original sources often took the form of average costs or resource utilization for various numbers of ships, so that each such number had to be converted to a first-ship basis. Because each average datum was originally calculated from a first-ship estimate using a so-called progress function, they could be revised to apply to the first ship by working backward along the function. A 93 percent average cost-progress curve was used for labor cost.[5] This rather steep progress function yielded first-ship costs which included the substantial shipyard outlays for design and engineering labor necessary to begin production. Because experience is expected to yield only minor savings of materials, a 98 percent curve was employed for materials cost.[6]

The manpower-planning estimates allow for more drafting and lofting labor to produce ships of entirely new designs than for ship types that have been built before. This labor input is mainly a set-up cost concentrated in the first ship produced. In working back to first-ship labor, therefore, a steeper, 90 percent progress curve was used for entirely new programs, while a 93.5 percent curve

Table B-1
Average Historical Labor Input Proportions by Phase of Construction

Ship Category	Hull Construction	Electrical Outfitting	Other Outfitting
Surface combatants	0.37	0.15	0.48
Submarines	0.46	0.14	0.40
Underway replenishment	0.50	0.07	0.43
Amphibious and auxiliary ships	0.44	0.12	0.44
Commercial ships	0.50	0.20	0.30

was applied to repeated designs. Table B-2 summarizes the progress functions used for adjustments of various data to a first-ship basis as well as those used subsequently to estimate average costs and resource-use rates for the model.

Because we wished to exclude drafting and lofting personnel from consideration, both 15 percent of the first-ship labor for new designs and 5 percent for repeat designs were then removed from the data.[7] An additional 25 percent of the remainder was deducted for all ships to exclude unskilled labor, leaving only directly allocable, blue-collar artisans.[8] This was the only class of labor to which the constraints apply.

B-3 Ways Time-Use Coefficients

The time on a building position required for a ship also is constrained. To derive ways-utilization coefficients for each ship in each qualified yard, first-ship ways periods in each yard were converted to averages for series of ships.

Estimates of the times on ways under the urgent conditions of mobilization have been made for various naval ships by the Business and Defense Services

Table B-2
Progress Functions for Calculating Costs and Resource-utilization Rates

Progress Function: $AC = \frac{F}{V^p}$

Variable	Percent Average Cost Decline Per Doubling of Output	Progress Exponent (p)
First-ship costs		
Labor cost	6.8	0.102
Materials cost	2.0	0.029
Overhead	0	–
First-ship labor hours†		
New ship designs	10.0	0.152
Repeat designs	6.5	0.097
Average coefficients for model use‡		
Costs	Same as for costs above	
Labor hours, all ships	6.8	0.102
Ways years	4.8	0.071

*In the formula, AC denotes average ship cost; F denotes first-ship cost; V indicates the cumulative volume of production; p is an exponent less than unity.

+These values were used in the preliminary processing to obtain standardized first-ship labor hours.

‡These values were employed to calculate average coefficients for production runs in the model, after adjustments for regional wage levels and yard equipment.

Agency.[9] The *relative* times for different ships were adopted from this study. Actual times were obtained by using as a basing point recent experience with destroyer escorts, for which 11 months from keel-laying to launch typified first-ship performance. For ships not included in the BDSA study (such as nuclear frigates, helicopter assault ships (LHAs), and merchant ships), we estimated first-ship ways use by comparing hull manpower inputs.

The coefficients of ways time use for each potential ship run in the model were obtained using the progress function given in Table B-2. This progress function was derived by regression analysis using data for multi-ship runs in the past.[10]

To differentiate ways periods by yard for each ship type, the average keel-to-launch time described above was adjusted to reflect differences in labor hours expended in hull erection at the building site. It was assumed that the ways period for a given ship would be proportional to the amount of hull labor used at the ways by the yard. This is equivalent to assuming that each yard uses the same size labor force at the ways. An index of hull-construction labor used at the ways in each yard was obtained by multiplying each yard's index of manpower use in hull construction (Table 3-3) by the fraction of its total hull labor employed at the ways (Table F-3). These index numbers were used to adjust the average first-ship ways time in each yard.

B-4 The Aggregation of Data for Certain Ships

Fifteen to seventeen actual ship types were grouped into 10 categories by genus (surface combatants, submarines, tankers, etc.), length, and the presence or absence of nuclear power. Two generic categories (amphibious and auxiliary) were merged because no significant difference was found historically between average labor input proportions for the two. For multi-ship categories, data for the individual ships on cost, labor utilization, and period on ways were averaged together, using as weights the number of ships of each type to be purchased.

Having arrived at standardized first-ship cost and resource-utilization coefficients for each ship category, we arrayed the coefficients by yard, using regional wage- and resource-utilization differentials. Then the cost curves were constructed with the help of progress functions, as described in Chapter 4. The resource-use rates are calculated similarly, as outlined in Chapter 3. The coefficients of the progress curves used to calculate the average costs and use coefficients for the model are shown in Table B-2.

Appendix C
The Processing of Yard Employment Data

The initial limitation on the amount of skilled shipyard production labor available was derived from 1967 skilled-employment levels. Only blue-collar labor was considered. This manpower was divided by examining craft designations into hull electrical work and nonelectrical outfitting work, respectively. These employment groupings correspond as closely as possible to the breakdown of labor requirements described in Appendix B. Labor devoted to repair and conversion activities (not dealt with in this report) were removed. The resulting employment levels provide the right-hand sides in the labor constraints shown in Appendix A.

C-1 The Employment Data

The available information on actual shipyard employment and its various components presents a picture of considerable diversity among yards. Especially diverse are the proportions in which skilled craftsmen were employed and the ratios of skilled workers to unskilled and overhead labor. Reasons for these divergences lie in different techniques of production, different degrees of capacity utilization, and different stages of completion of shipbuilding in process at the time of the observation. Firms with highly automated procedures showed high ratios of overhead to blue-collar personnel. Yards with declining workloads and excess capacity probably showed high ratios of skilled to unskilled employees because of the practice of retaining the former when orders taper off while dismissing the latter. A yard in the initial phase of a large program could be expected to have a higher proportion of hull-construction labor, while one approaching termination of a program would have more outfitting and electrical labor on hand.

Unfortunately, the confidential nature of much of the employment information prohibits presentation of a thorough analysis of the data. Tests indicate, as stated in Section 3-2 that the distortions embodied in these data do not affect the outcome of the linear program significantly.

C-2 Grouping of Skilled Employment by Function

Shipyard skilled employment was grouped for the model constraints into work forces devoted mainly to hull construction, electrical installations, and nonelectrical installations, respectively. According to our groupings, 50 percent of the workmen were employed on the hull, 38 percent on propulsion, auxiliary equipment, outfitting and armaments, and 12 percent—exclusively electricians—on the installation of the electrical system and the command and control equipment.

Close inspection of the craft definitions indicated that cases of overlap between groupings by craft and groupings by phase of construction were neither frequent nor serious. For instance, the welding of pipe (an outfitting job) is the function of a pipefitter and not of a welder. The welding of sheet metal is done by the sheetmetal worker. These definitions permit the classification of welders almost exclusively as hull workers. On the other hand, even though painters work on both the hull and outfitting, all painting was classed in the labor-use categorization as outfitting. Such unavoidable classification errors are not likely to alter the ranking of the model's cost coefficients nor to affect the solution values.

C-3 Exclusion of Workers for Conversion and Repair from Shipyard Employment

Several of the shipyards represented in the model conducted no conversion or repair activities. For the others, however, it was necessary to eliminate the skilled manpower devoted to this work to arrive at the labor force available for new ships.

The amount of conversion and repair has changed very erratically in each yard over time and showed no trend. Having no basis for estimating future levels of conversion and repair for the yards in question, we simply deducted the estimated manpower used for them in 1967 (the latest data year).

An estimate for each yard of the man-hours of skilled production workers in conversion and repair in 1967 was obtained by dividing 1967 receipts from this business by the ratio of shipyard receipts per skilled man-hour. This ratio was obtained in several steps from data in the 1963 *Census of Manufacturers.*[1] The resulting numbers were deducted from each yard's labor force without changing the 1967 skill distribution.

Appendix D
Production Functions, Labor Supply, and the Costs of Output Expansion

The cost data described in Appendix B are based on government planning estimates. These estimates, however, were sufficient only to determine the downward portion of the cost curve. They did not provide a means of estimating the cost of expansion beyond the minimum point on the cost curve. Beyond this point, production can be expanded only by using less efficient combinations of men and machinery, raising marginal cost of output. Higher labor costs also are encountered due to overtime and shift pay, costs of training new people or of bidding them away from other work, or a combination of these things. It was necessary to take into account all these possibilities in approximating the rising section of the cost function.

D-1 Production Functions

The basic shape of the cost curve was determined by the underlying production function for the firm. If we assume that the supply of all factors is infinitely elastic at a given price and that the production function is linear homogeneous, then the *total* cost curve is a straight line radiating from the origin. Turning to Figure D-1, if labor were substituted for quantity of output (the customary label) on the horizontal axis of the cost diagram, and if the ratio of capital to labor were kept constant, the total cost curve would look like OA. The corresponding marginal cost curve would be horizontal line AA' in Figure D-2. If the assumption of infinite elasticity of supply of the capital factor is now dropped (with that pertaining to labor retained) in favor of the assumption that there is some fixed amount of plant and equipment in place, which we shall call K_0, then a new set of cost curves can be derived. Since only one quantity of labor, L_0, can be optimal with the capital K_0, the new total cost curve must lie everywhere above the old one except at the point L_0 where they are tangent. This new curve is shown in Figure D-1 as the line BC. The marginal and average cost curves derived from it are labeled MC and AVC, respectively, in Figure D-2. The marginal cost curve clearly must cross the line AA' at the point L_0. The average cost curve is also tangent to AA' at this point.

The assumptions underlying the derivation of the minimum point on the average cost curve (as discussed in Chapter 3-3) were the same as those upon which this analysis is based. The point was assumed to be the point of optimal utilization of labor for a given investment in plant and equipment. Thus, the basic ship cost coefficients derived for each of the shipyards presumably correspond to this point on their respective cost curves.

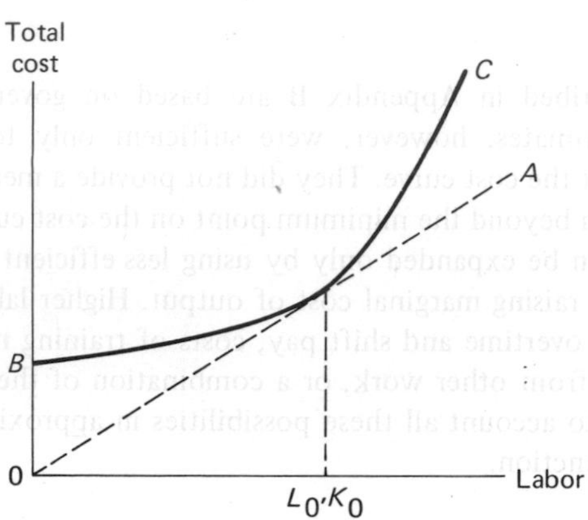

Figure D–1. Total-cost curve.

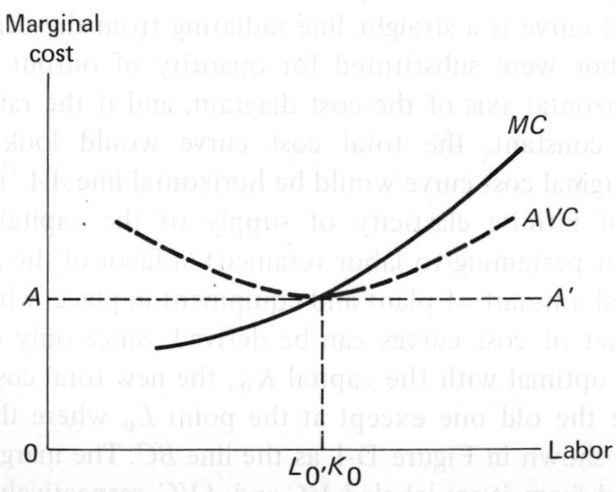

Figure D–2. Marginal and average cost curves.

If the form and parameters of the production function were known, it would be possible to estimate the locations of the cost curves in Figure D-2, given that the amount of the capital input is known. There is apparently only one study available that attempts to derive the necessary information. That was a study done by Resource Management Corporation for the Naval Ship Systems Command.[1] The RMC study concludes that the production function can be approximated by a linear homogeneous function of the Cobb-Douglas form. In other words, it is of the form

$$V = AL^{a}K^{\beta} \qquad a + \beta = 1 \tag{D-1}$$

where V is value added, L is labor input, K is capital input, and A is a size and unit coefficient. The RMC estimates of a and β are 0.796 and 0.271, respectively.

It is appropriate at this point to derive the general relationship that exists between changes in output and changes in marginal costs for a Cobb-Douglas production function. If we assume that capital is fixed at K_0, the production function is

$$V = AL^{a}K_0^{\beta} \tag{D-2}$$

If we let w equal the wage rate and r equal the return to capital, then total costs (exclusive of materials) are

$$TC = wL + rK_0 \qquad \text{(D-3–}$$

If we solve Equation (D-2) for L, we get

$$L = \left(\frac{V}{AK_0^{\,1-a}}\right)^{1/a} \tag{D-2$'$}$$

Upon substituting Equation (D-2′) for L in Equation (D-3), we obtain

$$TC = w\left(\frac{V}{AK_0^{\,1-a}}\right)^{1/a} + rK_0 \tag{D-4}$$

When Equation (D-4) is differentiated with respect to V, we get the marginal cost, which is

$$\frac{\partial TC}{\partial V} = \frac{w}{a(AK_0^{\,1-a})^{1/a}} V^{\frac{(1-a)}{a}} = \frac{w}{a(AK_0^{\,1-a})^{1/a}} V^{\beta/a} \tag{D-5}$$

If we wished to obtain the absolute value of marginal cost from this formula alone, it would be necessary to know the values for all parameters on the right-hand side of the equation. Since we already have estimates of the marginal ship cost for one quantity, however, we need only a ratio to determine that for another. Let MC_0 be the minimum point on the average cost curve and MC_1 be the marginal cost for any other quantity. The ratio between the two is then given by:

$$\frac{MC_1}{MC_0} = \frac{wV_1^{\beta/a}}{a(AK_0^{1-a})^{1/a}} \bigg/ \frac{wV_0^{\beta/a}}{a(AK_0^{1-a})^{1/a}} = \left(\frac{V_1}{V_0}\right)^{\beta/a} \qquad \text{(D-6)}$$

Thus, if $\beta = 0.271$ and $a = 0.796$, then $\beta/a \approx 1/3$. If we wished to know the ratio of marginal costs for a 30 percent increase in output, we would have

$$\frac{MC_1}{MC_0} = (1.3)^{1/3} \approx 1.1$$

In other words, a 30 percent increase in production gives a 10 percent increase in marginal cost.

One important assumption that we have made throughout is that the price elasticity of labor is infinite. Thus, the wage rates in the numerator and denominator of Equation (D-6) are the same and therefore cancel out. If the wage rate is likely to be different at different outputs, however, then Equation (D-6) becomes:

$$\frac{MC_1}{MC_0} = \frac{w_1}{w_0}\left(\frac{V_1}{V_0}\right)^{\beta/a} \qquad \text{(D-6')}$$

D-2 Labor-supply Elasticity

Determining the ratio of marginal costs now requires that the elasticity of the labor-supply curve be estimated. If we let E be this elasticity, it can be defined as:

$$E = \frac{\Delta W}{\Delta L} \frac{L_0}{W_0} \qquad \text{(D-7)}$$

Let

$$\Delta W = W_1 - W_0$$

$$\Delta L = L_1 - L_0$$

$$W_1 - W_0 = E \frac{W_0}{L_0} (L_1 - L_0)$$

$$\frac{W_1}{W_0} = E \frac{L_1}{L_0} - E + 1 \qquad \text{(D-8)}$$

Substituting Equation (D-8) into Equation (D-6′), we get

$$\frac{MC_1}{MC_0} = \left(\frac{V_1}{V_0}\right)^{\beta/a} (E \frac{L_1}{L_0} - E + 1 \qquad \text{(D-9)}$$

It is now necessary to substitute for L_1 / L_0. From Equation (D-2′),

$$\frac{L_1}{L_0} = \left(\frac{V_1}{V_0}\right)^{1/a}$$

$$\frac{MC_1}{MC_0} = \left(\frac{V_1}{V_0}\right)^{\beta/a} \left[E \left(\frac{V_1}{V_0}\right)^{\frac{\beta+1}{a}} - E + 1\right]$$

$$\frac{MC_1}{MC_0} = \left(\frac{V_1}{V_0}\right)^{\beta/a} + E \left[\left(\frac{V_1}{V_0}\right)^{\frac{\beta+1}{a}} - \left(\frac{V_1}{V_0}\right)^{\beta/a}\right] \qquad \text{(D-9′)}$$

$$\frac{MC_1}{MC_0} = (1 - E) \frac{V_1}{V_0}^{\beta/a} + E \frac{V_1}{V_0}^{(\beta+1)/a}$$

Again using the values $\beta = 0.271$, $a = 0.796$, $\beta/a \approx 1/3$ and $(\beta+1)/a \approx 3/2$, the ratio of marginal costs for a 30 percent increase in output is

$$\frac{MC_1}{MC_0} = (1 - E)(1.3)^{1/3} + E(1.3)^{3/2}$$

If we let $E = 0.26$, the ratio is[2]

$$\frac{MC_1}{MC_0} \approx 0.74\,(1.1) + 0.26\,(1.46) \approx 1.19$$

Thus, using an assumption of wage elasticity of 0.26, a 30 percent increase in production results in approximately a 20 percent increase in marginal costs as compared with the 10 percent increase without the upward-sloping labor-supply curve.

Equation (D-9′) was used to derive the marginal-cost ratios for this study. The ratio is a function of the increase in production (or the increase in labor used). Since the marginal cost is an increasing function of production, the ratio is also a continuous function. It was approximated by calculating the ratio at three points. These points were for a 30, 60, and 100 percent increase in production beyond the minimum-cost point. The values of the ratios are, of course, identical for all yards since they were based on percentage increases in production. The ratios of the increased marginal costs to the minimum cost are 1.19 for a 30 percent increase, 1.38 for a 60 percent increase, and 1.64 for a 100 percent increase.

Since an increase in output is linearly related to an increase in labor input in the model, it was necessary to convert the costs in terms of ships to a cost per man-hour. In addition, since each yard is capable of producing a number of different types of ships which use different proportions of each class of labor, it was necessary to use a weighted average in calculating the cost per hour of increasing production via labor-force increases. Thus, the total labor cost for each ship at the point of optimal production was divided by the number of man-hours required to produce that ship to arrive at a cost per man-hour. These man-hour costs were averaged over all ships that could be built in the yard to arrive at an average figure. The average man-hour cost for each yard was then multiplied by the percentage increase in marginal cost for the 30, 60, and 100 percent increase in production levels to obtain the figures actually used in the program as the costs of increasing production via increases in the labor force. These costs are shown in Table D-1.

Table D-1
Labor Expansion Costs ($/man-hour)

Yard	Percent Increase in Production 30	60	100
1	0.769	1.528	2.540
2	0.780	1.552	2.580
3	0.819	1.628	2.707
4	0.855	1.700	2.826
5	0.848	1.687	2.804
6	0.777	1.544	2.567
7	0.941	1.871	3.110
8	1.028	2.044	3.398
9	0.797	1.584	2.634
10	0.951	1.890	3.142
11	0.911	1.812	3.012
12	0.733	1.457	2.421
13	0.695	1.381	2.296
14	0.828	1.646	2.735
15	0.785	1.561	2.595

Appendix E Economics of Splitting Ship Runs Among Yards

All the original calculations of minimum ship costs and resource utilization in construction were made under the assumption that each yard, if it produced any ship type, would either produce this ship at the minimum-cost output rate for its facilities or produce the total quantity demanded if the total were less than sufficient to occupy the minimum-cost capacity. Implicit in both of these parameter calculations is the assumption that the participation of every yard building a particular ship type continues for the duration of the procurement of this ship type by the buyer.

E-1 Inconsistency between Cost Coefficients and Ship Awards

In running the program, however, two related problems appear which cause the number of ships built in a yard to be less than the number for which the cost and resource-utilization coefficients were calculated. Thus, the solution is not consistent with the data inputs because the prices in the program are calculated from a lower point on the cost-progress curve than they should be for the number of ships in the production run. First, this inconsistency can arise when all participating yards are producing for the duration of the buyer's procurements, either because large purchases are divided among several yards or because some yards undertake the work on the upward-sloping portion of their marginal-cost functions. Second, this inconsistency can occur if efficient yards excel at producing ship types for which the demand terminates after one or two model periods, enabling them in later periods to win parts of other jobs from higher-cost firms.

One way of correcting this discrepancy would be to adjust the prices in each producing yard to the appropriate level for the number of ships produced and then calculate a new solution. (It also would be necessary to adjust the prices in yards not originally allocated ships in order to be certain they do not enter the new solution.) Determining an equilibrium ship allocation in this way may require solving for more than one set of price adjustments.

In addition to the iterative approach of adjusting ship cost coefficients to the production runs assigned in a previous solution until consistency is attained, it would be possible simply to impose a constraint such that no yard is permitted to build a ship in a later period unless it built the same type of ship in the previous period. It also would be possible to use the iterative approach for some cases and a constraint for others. Which of these two methods is considered appropriate depends on the relative efficiency of different ways of allocating the number of ships demanded. If it is more efficient to allocate all ships in one contract, then it makes good sense to restrict production of each ship type to one yard (except for those cases where demand is so great that one yard cannot handle the total). If, however, there are benefits from spreading production among yards, either at a point in time by letting several small contracts at once, or over time by letting several smaller contracts in successive time periods, then constraints restricing production to a single yard should not be included.[1]

A constraint preventing a yard from producing a ship not previously produced in that yard does not prevent the buy from being broken up into several small contracts at a point in time. Similarly, a constraint that permits only one or two yards to produce a given ship at a point in time does not prevent shifting to a different yard to the following time period.

E-2 Splitting Production between two Yards

We now turn to an analysis of circumstances under which it is cheaper to produce in two yards than in one, given that the costs in one yard are below those in the other. In a two-yard model, if the cheaper yard has the capacity and we are looking only at costs for a single ship type, it will be cheaper to produce everything in the less expensive yard. However, if because it is already building one ship type, this yard has only limited capacity remaining for construction of other ships, there are two alternatives, either of which might turn out to be the best, depending upon absolute costs and the learning-curve parameters. One possibility is to split production of the second ship type between the two yards, and the other is to produce everything in the more expensive yard.

Suppose we let TC_1 be the cost of producing some given number of ships V in yard 1 which has higher costs than yard 2. Then we have

$$TC_1 \quad = \quad A_1 V^{(1-\beta)} \tag{E-1}$$

where A_1 is the cost of producing the first ship and b is the average cost learning-curve coefficient. The cost of producing in both yards is

$$TC_{\text{Splitrun}} = A_1 V_1^{(1-\beta)} + A_2 V_2^{(1-\beta)} \tag{E-2}$$

with

$$V_1 + V_2 = V$$

The point at which the two total-cost curves cross is $TC_1 = TC_2$, or

$$A_1 V^{(1-\beta)} = A_1 V_1^{(1-\beta)} + A_2 V_2^{(1-\beta)} \tag{E-3}$$

Unfortunately this equation cannot be solved explicitly for V_1 or V_2 as a function of the other parameters. It is possible, however, to solve for a range of values for V_2 and V_1 for a given V and thus determine the range over which one solution or the other would be the best. This has been done using $A_2 = 100$ and $V = 100$ and ranging A_1 from 100 to 135 and V_2 from zero to 100. The total-cost curve for a split run looks like that in Figure E-1.

TC_1 is the cost of building all ships in yard 1, and TC_2 is the cost of building them all in yard 2. The horizontal axis is the number of ships out of a total of 100 that are built in yard 2. In the example shown in Figure E-1, yard 2 would have to have capacity available to produce at least q ships before it would pay to permit it to build any. For any mix assigning fewer than q to yard 2, it is cheaper to have all the ships built in yard 1, in spite of the fact that it is the higher-cost yard.

Although the solutions are derived for specific values of V_1, A_1, and A_2, it is a fairly simple matter to obtain some coefficients that permit them to be converted to any values of these variables. The solution value for the ratio between V_2 and V, at the point where TC_1 and TC_2 are equal, is invariant with respect to the total value of V for a given ratio between A_2 and A_1. This can be

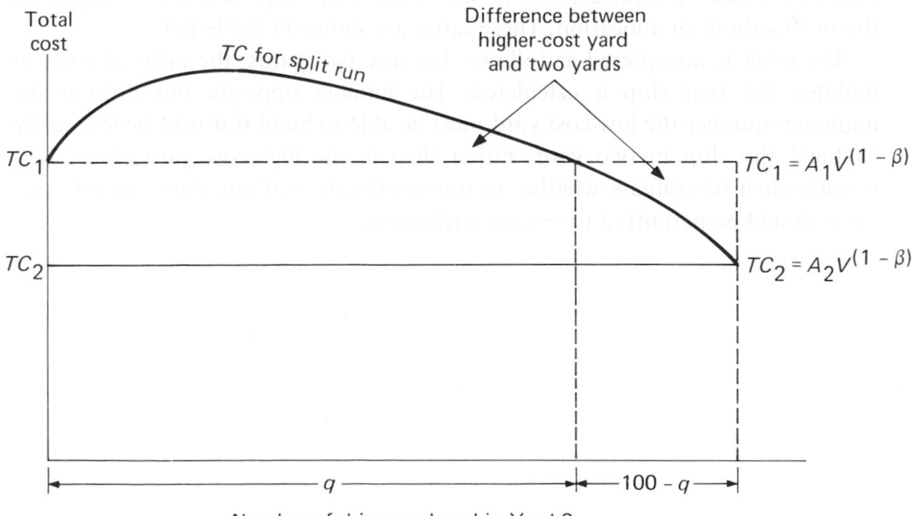

Figure E–1. Comparison of total-cost curve for building in one yard and building in two yards.

demonstrated as follows: Suppose we let D be the difference between single-run and split-run costs:

$$D = A_1 V^{(1-\beta)} - A_1 V_1{}^{(1-\beta)} - A_2 V_2{}^{(1-\beta)}$$

$$= A_1 \left(V^{(1-\beta)} - V_1{}^{(1-\beta)} - \frac{A_2}{A_1} V_2{}^{(1-\beta)} \right)$$

$$= A_1 V^{(1-\beta)} \left[1 - \left(\frac{V_1}{V}\right)^{(1-\beta)} - \frac{A_2}{A_1} \left(\frac{V_2}{V}\right)^{(1-\beta)} \right]$$

At D equals 0 the total production costs are equal for both methods of allocation. At the same time, if A_1 and V are not zero, the D equals 0 only if the part of the right-hand side of the equation in brackets is zero. But the parentheses contain only ratios, so that once the condition-satisfying ratios of V_1/V and V_2/V are found for a given value of A_2/A_1, these ratios are valid regardless of the level of V. The solution is also independent of the absolute levels of A_2 and A_1 once their ratio is given.

Only the absolute value of the cost difference is affected by changing the number of ships required, V_1, or the level of costs, A_1 and A_2 (as long as the latter are changed proportionately so that their ratio is constant). Thus, solving the system for a single value of V and the entire range of feasible cost ratios yields the range of volume ratios at which the costs of production are equal for the two methods of allocation. These ratios are shown in Table E-1.

The table is interpreted as follows. For any two yards, the ratio of costs of building the first ship is calculated. The number opposite this ratio is the minimum number the low-cost yard must be able to build if it is to be less costly to build the ship in two yards rather than in the high-cost yard alone. It is possible then to evaluate whether or not an allocation of one ship type into two yards should be permitted to remain unchanged.

Table E-1
Equal-cost Point for Single and Split-run Ship Allocations

First-Ship Cost Ratio A_1/A_2	% in Low-Cost Yard*	First-Ship Cost Ratio A_1/A_2	% in Low-cost Yard
1.00	–	1.18	27
1.01	98	1.19	24
1.02	94	1.20	22
1.03	90	1.21	20
1.04	85	1.22	18
1.05	80	1.23	16
1.06	75	1.24	15
1.07	70	1.25	13
1.08	65	1.26	12
1.09	60	1.27	11
1.10	56	1.28	10
1.11	51	1.29	9
1.12	47	1.30	8
1.13	43	1.31	8
1.14	39	1:32	7
1.15	35	1.33	6
1.16	32	1.34	6
1.17	29	1.35	5

*This is the minimum fraction of the total volume the low-cost yard must be able to build before the split run is less costly.

Appendix F
Yard Technology and Investment

To translate each yard's comparative advantage in the production of ships into meaningful units of measure, it was necessary to take an inventory of each yard's capital stock. This was accomplished in the following steps:

1. Selecting the critical production functions in the ship-construction process
2. Identifying the type and capacity of the capital equipment immediately available to each yard for performing each function
3. Deriving labor-productivity differences for each yard from an analysis of the equipment in the yard by estimating the man-hour requirements for constructing a specific ship.

F-1 Hull-construction Process

It is convenient to think of the shipbuilding process as consisting of three stages:

1. The preparation of pieces of metal for assembly into hull sections
2. The integration of these sections in a building dock, shipways, or on a platform
3. The installation of machinery and equipment in the ship

The three stages of the process vary in relative importance not only with the type of ship being built but also with the character and layout of the shipyard.

The most capital-intensive of the three stages in a modern yard is preparation of plates and beams and their assembly into hull sections. This stage together with the integration of these sections make up the hull-construction phase of shipbuilding. Figure F-1 shows details of the hull-construction process in a diagram of the flow of production.

The steel-preparation subprocess involves two separate procedures (see Figure F-1): (1) the procurement, sorting, and retrieving of plates and beams and their cleaning and priming prior to cutting and bending; and (2) the design of hull components and the transfer of the engineering drawings (lofting) by one of several methods onto the plates or beams.

The steel-processing function refers to (1) the flame-cutting of plates and beams and (2) bending and flanging of plates according to design. Finally, some plates are welded into larger panels before being removed to the assembly area.

The assembly subprocess is perhaps the least capital-intensive function of U.S. shipyards. Plates and sections are welded into place, and units are fused into

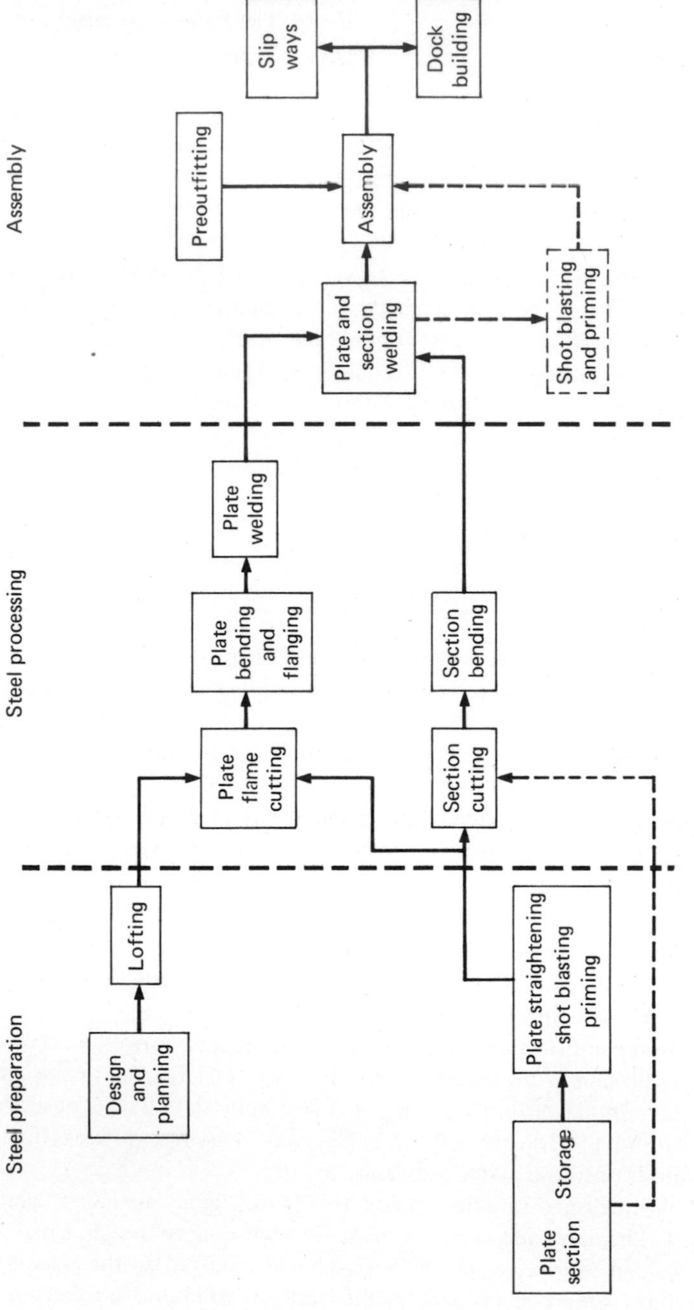

Figure F–1. The hull-erection process.

large modules, the size of which is a function of available crane lift capability. In many shipyards some of the preoutfitting starts here before the module is lifted or rolled onto the ways, platform, or dock. Once in the integration area, where modules and sections are fused into an integrated whole, heavy machinery, equipment, and deck houses are moved into place.

When the integration process is complete, the hull is launched and floated to a pier where outfitting is finished. The time at the outfitting pier is a direct function of the amount of preoutfitting completed before launching.

F-2 Hull-erection Productivity

Because the hull-erection portion of the shipbuilding process is the most capital-intensive of the several construction stages, it is here that labor-productivity differences among the yards emerge most clearly. These differentials are expressed for each yard in terms of man-hours per ship for each ship type compared with a certain representative yard.

It was impossible to inventory all capital equipment at every yard; therefore, we selected only those production functions in which man-hour savings from capital-intensive as opposed to labor-intensive methods are the greatest. Table 3-1 shows the major innovations in steel processing equipment and the labor savings available from new equipment compared with the least efficient process now in use. For example, a yard with the most modern capital facilities has a fully computerized plate-preparation system, i.e., numerical fairing and lofting and tape-controlled drafting. In addition, the yard stores its plates horizontally and retrieves them with a crane that can lift both steel and aluminum plates—the former with a magnet, the latter with suction cups. Plate processing also is done mechanically, i.e., with a smoothing and painting machine. Plate cutting is integrated with the numerical lofting process. Numerical tapes prepared in the lofting shop are fed into the cutting machines which automatically direct the torches to cut plates into numerically described shapes. As shown in Table 3-1, labor savings from recent innovations are substantial. However, while saving labor, these methods involve larger capital costs.

Fairing and lofting in yards using older techniques continue to be done manually, and the draftsmen are assisted by a drafting machine with a drawing speed of less than 50 inches per minute. Plates still are stored vertically and are retrieved by riggers with the help of overhead cranes. Several yards continue to use some or all of these techniques. Some yards still smooth and prime plates manually, and one other yard continues to cut plates with full-scale, mainly manual methods.

Table F-1 indicates a qualitative judgment of the degree to which old steel-processing methods had been supplanted with new equipment by 1968. Three yards have invested large amounts in renovating their already better than

Table F-1
Modernization of Steel-processing Equipment in U.S. Shipyards (by region, 1968)

Extent of Equipment Modernization	Number of Yards East Coast*	Gulf Coast	West Coast
Largely modernized	2	1	0
Partially modernized	3	1	1
Slightly modernized	3	1	2

*This region includes one yard located on Lake Michigan.

average facilities. Five yards, although up-to-date in a number of steel-processing functions, have yet to modernize and integrate their production processes fully. Six yards have replaced little or no equipment recently.

To combine each yard's relative manpower use in each subprocess into an aggregate for the entire hull-construction process in a way permitting comparisons among yards, it is necessary first to establish "weights" for each function based on some representative yard. These weights are the proportions of the representative yard's hull-labor inputs devoted to each subprocess. The average distribution of man-hours for constructing four different ships at a representative yard is shown in Table F-2. Only 15 percent of total hull-erection man-hours in a representative yard were used in plate-processing functions for which productivity differences were considered. Productivity differences for assembly of ship sections and for outfitting are gauged from lifting capacity, as outlined below.

By multiplying the fraction of hull labor devoted to plate cutting in the representative yard by the proportion of this yard's cutting labor devoted to cutting in another yard, we obtain the latter yard's cutting labor as a fraction of the representative yard's total hull-labor requirement. The sum of these products for all subprocesses gives total hull requirements in the second yard as a fraction of total requirements in the representative yard.[1]

The results of summing these products are displayed in Table 3-3. Table F-3 shows the distribution of each yard's labor inputs as proportions of its total hull inputs. The savings through recent innovations in equipment are mainly in the realm of preliminary processing rather than in functions carried out at the platens and ways. The table indicates that the yards with the most modern equipment expend the highest proportion of hull labor at these building areas, reducing labor for preliminary processing to less than 10 percent of total hull-construction manpower.

F-3 Outfitting Productivity

Hull erection and outfitting, although clearly different, are nonetheless interwoven for a considerable portion of the construction period. This integration of

Table F-2
Man-hour Distribution by Hull-erection Function in a Representative Yard*

Function	Percent Hull Labor in Each Function
Preliminary processing	
Fairing and Lofting	9
Drafting	1
Plate Storage and Retrieval	1
Plate Smoothing and Priming	1
Plate Cutting	3
Subtotal	15
Assembly and erection	
Welding	21
Fitting (at ways and on platens)	43
Chipping and grinding	8
Steel fairing	2
Erection and material handling	5
Riveting	2
Subtotal	81
Miscellaneous	4
Total	100

*This distribution is calculated from data for four ship types in a representative American yard.

one activity into the other takes on particular significance when preoutfitting is started early in the ship construction period and carried out extensively.

Industry opinion as to the merits of using preoutfitting in U.S. naval construction is divided, but the concensus holds that preoutfitting is desirable and that resulting cost savings can be substantial. The extent of preassembly and preoutfitting that is feasible depends heavily on capacity to lift sections of the ship onto the building positions. As outlined in Chapter 3, productivity in both hull erection and outfitting are made a function in this report of crane lifting capability for these purposes, using the judgment of shipbuilding experts as a guide in quantifying the function.

Although no American yards match the European and Japanese concerns in lifting capacity at present, maximum ways-side lift ranges from 50 to about 200 tons in the existing yards. The unweighted average of maximum-lift capabilities in existing yards is about 100 tons. The new yard in Mississippi is expected to have cranes capable of hoisting 400 tons at a time. The estimated savings in manpower for hull integration and outfitting through larger cranes are indicated in Table 3-2.

Outfitting man-hour costs, much more than full-erection costs, are affected by factors such as the following which have defied proper quantification:

1. The prompt or delayed arrival of ship components, especially shipboard equipment
2. Frequent and/or delayed orders to change equipment or ship design
3. Naval standards for shock and stress resistance, quality and finish

The quantitative influence of these problems remains a promising field for further research in understanding defense costs.

Table F-3
Distribution of each Yard's Hull-erection Labor by Construction Function (In Percent of Total Erection Labor)

Yard	Fairing and Lofting	Drafting	Plate Handling	Plate Processing	Plate Cutting	Ways and Other Hull-erection Labor
1	01.2	00.0	01.9	00.8	03.3	92.8
2	00.7	00.0	01.1	00.5	01.9	95.6
3	02.0	00.0	01.1	00.4	01.9	94.6
4	00.7	00.0	01.2	00.6	02.0	95.5
5	09.8	00.5	01.0	00.4	01.8	86.5
6	09.5	00.5	01.0	00.6	03.4	85.0
7	09.4	00.5	01.0	00.4	03.4	85.4
8	16.1	00.5	01.0	00.6	03.2	78.6
9	07.9	00.4	00.8	16.1	02.8	71.9
10	09.2	00.5	01.0	00.9	03.3	85.2
11	11.4	00.3	04.5	13.0	11.5	59.3
12	08.0	00.4	05.6	00.6	14.2	71.2
13	11.5	00.3	04.5	13.1	11.5	59.1
14	11.8	00.0	04.6	13.4	11.8	58.4
15	09.9	00.5	06.9	00.4	03.5	78.7

Appendix G Conversion of Lump-sum Investment Costs to Periodic Rental Charges

The cost of investment in new equipment must be varied from period to period to take account of the fact that the model has only a finite horizon. From the point of view of the model, a piece of equipment purchased in the final period has a useful life of only one period, whereas if purchased in the first period it could be used for three periods. Putting the same cost on the equipment in all three periods would distort the true investment options.

In order to overcome this problem, it was necessary to convert the lump-sum cost of an equipment purchased into what might be called a periodic rental fee and then reconvert this into a lump-sum cost that is a function of the number of periods the equipment could be used in the model.

Since the equipment must be expected to earn a certain rate of return if it is to be purchased, this rate of return is the figure that was used to calculate the periodic rental payment that would be the equivalent of a lump-sum present expenditure. The formula for calculating present value is

$$P = A \sum_{i=0}^{n} \frac{1}{(1 + r)^i}$$

where P is the present value of lump-sum cost of an investment project, A is the periodic payment necessary to amortize the cost assuming no residual value (it is A that we shall call the rental), r is the rate of return on investment, and n is the number of periods the equipment can be expected to last. If the equation is solved for A, we have

$$A = P \frac{1}{\sum_{i=0}^{n} (1 + r)^{-i}} = \frac{Pr}{1 - (1 + r)^{-n}}$$

A, then, is the periodic cost to the firm of having the equipment available. In calculating the value for A, we shall assume that r equals 20 percent, which is approximately the average before-tax rate of return on investment in the private economy, and that n equals 12 years. Thus, for a \$100,000 investment,[1]

$$A = \frac{\$100{,}000 \times 0.20}{1 - (1.10)^{-12}} = \frac{\$20{,}000}{0.6812} = \$22{,}500$$

Since investment always involves a lump-sum payment in the model, the annual rentals must be converted to a lump sum that is equal to the present value of future payments over the life of the investment. If P_n is the lump-sum cost of a \$100,000 investment with a remaining life in the model of n years, we have

$$P_n = \sum_{i=1}^{n} \frac{A}{(1+r)^i}$$

Since investment in the first period has a life of 12 years, P_n for Period I is \$100,000. For Period II in which investment has a life of eight years, P_8 is \$86,332. And in Period III with only four years to run, P_4 is \$58,230.[2]

Appendix H
Calculation of the Savings from Investment

In attempting to establish each yard's prospective investment function, we selected specific construction subprocesses for which equipment could be updated. For each subprocess we determined what equipment could be added that the yard did not already have. Next, we measured the desirability of adding this equipment in terms of potential savings in shipbuilding labor cost. Each yard determines whether or not to buy the equipment, depending on whether these savings outweigh the cost. The upper limit of equipment buys is that set by the latest available technology in each subprocess.

Since some yards already possess new equipment, not all are candidates for investment in each equipment type. Nor is it necessary for each yard to invest the same amount as any other yard in a given type to provide the required capacity or level of technology. This is particularly true of cranes. Conversely, some investments, such as plate processing, are less divisible in cost than others but satisfy a wide range of capacity needs. As a result, they may provide higher returns for large yards than for small ones.

Certain complementaries of investments exist in shipbuilding; for instance, it is unlikely that a shipyard would invest in numerical fairing without at the same time obtaining a numerical lofting and drafting capability. These interrelationships, therefore, were also considered in arriving at the prospective investment packages encompassed in the program.

In this appendix, the purchase prices of the new equipment in question are presented. Then the method of deriving man-hour savings is discussed. The man-hour savings are then translated to dollars of reduction in labor cost per $100,000 of equipment investment. This is the form into which savings coefficients are placed for the model.

H-1 The Costs of Steel Handling Equipment and Cranes

A simplified method of determining the costs of new equipment and facilities for each of the 15 shipyards had to be found. We decided to identify and estimate the costs of relatively homogeneous equipment only and to disregard all auxillary costs. The latter vary too much from yard to yard to permit even a rough approximation. The costs of the equipment shown in Table H-1, therefore, represent only the purchase prices of the key machinery and equipment.

Table H-1
Estimated Purchase Prices of Steel-processing Equipment and Cranes

Item	Price
Optically controlled fairing and Lofting Equipment	$ 80,000
Numerically controlled fairing equipment with Antokon-software (for surface ships only)	130,000
Drafting machine (Model 2637)	120,000
(Model 1215)	80,000
Plate yard (15 tons),* crane and normal conveyors (colocator or captivator not included)	300,000
Plate cleaning and priming equipment	300,000
Steel cutting Optically controlled,	250,000
Numerically controlled†	280,000
Conversion of optically to numerically controlled steel cutting	80,000
200-ton crane	540,000

*Minimum economic throughput per year is about 15,000 tons, but the equipment can handle up to 40,000 tons annually.

†One machine for every 4,000 tons of plates per year.

H-2 Potential Man-hour and Cost Savings from Investments

The savings from investment in each potential improvement in equipment were calculated. These savings are expressed as fractions of total hull-erection man-hours and of outfitting man-hours, where applicable. Table H-2 shows the number of yards which might become customers for each type of equipment, together with the range of labor savings and the average saving. The savings differ because of the diverse capital stocks on which total labor inputs are based and–in the cases of numerically controlled fairing, lofting, plate cutting, and cranes–because the labor savings are based on different original equipment in these functions.

Comparison of the new equipment with diverse pieces of old equipment, gives especially large ranges of savings for these items. In the case of plate cutting, for instance, the range of savings (roughly 1 to 13 percent of hull labor) encompasses conversion from manual guidance as well as from optically guided systems. The replacement of steel-processing equipment has no effect on outfitting-labor productivity. Only the cranes are relevant to this phase of the

Table H-2
Manpower Savings from Investments in Steel-processing Equipment and Cranes

Type of Equipment	Number of Interested Yards	Man-hour Savings: Hull Range	Hull Average	Outfitting Range	Outfitting Average
		(Percent of Hull Labor)		(Percent of Outfitting Labor)	
Fairing and lofting					
Optically controlled	3	5.0– 7.4	5.9		
Numerically controlled	10	7.4–15.5	9.7		
Numerically controlled Drafting	10	3.0– 5.0	4.4		
Plate yard	5	3.8– 5.9	4.4		
Plate cleaning and priming	4	12.8–15.7	13.4		
Plate cutting					
Optically controlled	4	9.2–11.4	9.8		
Numerically controlled	9	1.4–12.8	4.8		
Ways-side Cranes*	13	3.4–10.8	6.8	5.0–20.5	14.0

*Savings are calculated for an increase in ways-side lifting capability to 200 tons from that presently in each yard.

process. The manpower savings for crane investments represent those from upgrading wayside lifting capability in all yards to a uniform 200 tons, the industry's present maximum.

The savings from new equipment, summarized in Table H-2 were calculated using information on manning reductions from Tables 3-1 and 3-2 of the text. For instance, an optically guided fairing and lofting system is shown there to require about 56 percent of the labor needed for full-scale fairing and lofting. Numerically controlled operations would employ only about 6 percent as many persons as the full-scale method. Thus, the conversion from optical to numerical guidance would save 50 of every 56 labor units, or 89 percent. When this percentage reduction is multiplied by the proportion of hull man-hours devoted to fairing and lofting in the yard in question, the product is the fraction of the yard's total man-hours for hull erection that can be saved by the investment in numerically controlled equipment. This procedure was followed in evaluating all investments that can be made in each of the 14 existing yards. The results are shown in summary form in Table H-2 to protect trade secrets and to obscure yard identities.

H-3 Savings per $100,000 of Investment

The percent labor savings calculated in Table H-2 were applied to absolute data on yard employment for hull construction and outfitting. The resulting savings in labor hours then were evaluated using an East Coast labor cost of $5 per hour (1968 wages plus estimated fringe benefits). For other regions, the wage is adjusted using the Maritime Administration regional index (see Table 4-1). For example, an investment by one Southern yard in numerical fairing and lofting equipment would reduce man-hour requirements for that function by an estimated 61,000 hours per year. At labor costs of $4.50 per hour, the gross savings are $275,000. Since the investment would cost an estimated $130,000 (1.3 investment "units"), the savings would be $211,000 per unit per year. If the firm builds enough ships to utilize such a system, therefore, the investment would be highly profitable.

Table H-3 shows the undiscounted savings per unit on all investments considered. The arrangement of the yards does not correspond to the numbering system used in the text. Investment in numerically controlled fairing and lofting systems appears to be the line of investment which is most profitable for a large number of firms. By comparing the sum of these annual savings for the expected economic life of the equipment with its purchase price, using the formula shown in Equation G-1, one could calculate the implied rate of return on the investment *r*. Using a simpler rule of thumb, one could calculate the recoupment period for the investment from these figures.

Table H-3
Estimated Annual Labor-cost Saving in Steel-processing Equipment per $100,000 of Investment ($ thousands)

	Fairing and Lofting			Plate	Plate	Plate Cutting	
Yard*	Optical	Numerical	Drafting	Handling	Processing	Optical	Numerical
1	–†	–	–	–	–	–	–
2	–	–	–	–	–	–	–
3	–	–	–	–	–	–	–
4	–	–	–	–	–	–	–
5	–	.575	035	–	–	–	–
6	–	1,611	099	–	–	–	504
7	–	1,711	068	–	–	–	353
8	575	769	028	–	–	–	131
9	–	300	015	–	275	–	090
10	–	592	039	–	–	–	188
11	279	370	011	057	188	165	165
12	–	211	013	058	–	202	171
13	208	256	008	039	126	108	113
14	–	–	–	180	595	–	–
15	–	765	045	210	–	–	235

*The arrangement of the yards does not correspond to the numbering system used in the text.
†–means no investment in that category at that yard.

Since any yard could upgrade its equipment to the technological level of the most modern existing yards, it is not surprising to find the greatest potential savings from investments in the least efficient yards. The modern yards are likely to devote their investment resources principally to the upgrading of their crane lift capability. The returns to each yard from installing cranes capable of lifting 200 tons are shown in Table H-4.

H-4 Probable Shipyard Investments

Capacity limitations inherent in the computer prevent the segregation of investments into more than three groups. Investment in cranes was grouped separately because it is the only type of investment in this model that generates savings in outfitting labor as well as hull-erection labor. In this way the effects on both kinds of labor could be taken into account individually.

The remaining equipment types were divided into two groups, primarily on the basis of differentials in return per dollar invested. Since some equipment is complementary, such as numerical fairing, lofting and flame cutting, and since it is unlikely that one would be purchased without the other, these were put in the same group even though the return on one taken by itself might be considerably less than that on the other.

Each yard had a limited capacity to utilize new equipment of each type. Thus

Table H-4
Estimated Annual Cost Savings Per $100,000 Investment in Upgrading Lift Capability to 200 Tons ($ thousands)

Yard	Investment Cost	Ways or Dock Labor	Outfitting Labor	Total
1	$ –	$ –	$ –	$ –
2	375	81	90	171
3	475	15	15	30
4	240	50	95	145
5	370	15	30	45
6	415	40	63	103
7	475	102	114	116
8	315	22	34	54
9	475	10	35	45
10	540	57	74	131
11	540	57	108	165
12	415	9	54	63
13	500	17	91	108
14	370	35	–	35
15	–	–	–	–

there was an upper limit to the amount of investment each yard was permitted to undertake. Since cost savings and efficiency differ among the three investment groups, it was necessary to constrain investments in each group separately. The value of the constraint is the total cost of the equipment in a given group that a yard could buy and utilize effectively.[1]

Once we had grouped the investments by yard, it was possible to calculate the average man-hour savings for each group. From these potential savings in labor, together with the regional wage rate, we then determined the dollar savings for each yard and the total investment of each kind necessary to satisfy fully the needs for modernization of the yard.

The next question that arises is how this potential saving is allocated among ship types. Clearly, the new investment can yield no reduction in costs if no ships are built. In addition, since the real savings are in terms of man-hours of hull-erection and outfitting labor, the amount of saving per ship will be a function of the absolute and relative amounts of labor used. Since these vary considerably across ship types, the saving will also vary.

The savings in man-hours were initially calculated as percentages of hull-erection and outfitting man-hours worked in the various yards. In determining how the savings are utilized in building ships, we applied these same percentages to the hull-erection and outfitting labor required for each ship type.

For the outfitting labor, this calculation was direct, since only one of the investment groups, the crane investment, resulted in savings in outfitting labor. Thus, if investment in increased crane lift capacity resulted in a 1 percent saving in total outfitting labor for that yard, the dollar savings per ship were calculated as 1 percent of the outfitting labor used in that ship multiplied by the wage rate.

The final aspect of the effect of investment on a yard's activities was the direct effect on the labor and time required to build a ship. The total labor savings were used to calculate the dollar savings. Ideally, the labor savings that result if a yard invests should be taken into account by adjusting the figures for the amount of labor required to build each ship type. However, internal adjustment of the coefficients is difficult to accomplish in the linear program. An alternative solution was to assume that the labor savings had the effect of increasing the total labor pool available. Since the constraint on labor supply is primarily to restrict the number of ships that can be built at a given cost, it makes no difference whether the limit is increased because fewer hours are required per ship or because more hours are apparently available, as long as the permitted expansion is the same.

Appendix I
Derivation of Capacity-utilization Quotas for Work-dispersion Policies

In Chapter 9 we evaluated six potential alternative policies for maintaining a mobilization capability in the shipbuilding industry, i.e., a larger industry then would be sustained by peacetime ship demand. These policies consisted of dispersing orders for new construction throughout all firms in the industry rather than allocating them to the most efficient firms only. Each of the 15 yards was therefore required to operate at some minimum percentage of its capacity.

The utilization quotas for the maximum dispersion policy were based on the national average rate of capacity utilization in the industry in the cost-minimizing solution of the model. This average utilization was calculated as the proportion of available ways time occupied in the industry is a whole. When the small shipbuilding program was concentrated in the most efficient yards, these yards utilized about 44, 41, and 27 percent of total industry capacity for each of the three time periods. If the same volume of work were to be reallocated equally across all yards, then each yard should be able to utilize at least these fractions of its ways time in building the needed ships. To assure feasibility of the policy, we reduced these values slightly to 40 percent for Periods I and II and 26 percent for Period III and applied them as the minimum levels of operation for each yard.

To define the second, less extensive work-dispersal policy, in which the most efficient yard is permitted to operate at full capacity with the rest of the demand allocated to other yards in proportion to capacity, we referred again to the results of the basic program. The amount of ways time used in the most efficient yard was subtracted from the total amount used in the industry. The remainder was divided by total industry capacity minus the most efficient yard's capacity. The new ratios were 31 percent for Periods I and II and 16 percent for Period III. These were the minimum levels of ways utilization that all yards had to satisfy. Similar calculations were made for the least extensive work-dispersal policy by subtracting the two most efficient yards' utilization and available capacities from the industry totals and proceeding as above.

Quotas for the maximum dispersion policy for the high level of demand were based on the original ratio of total industry utilization to total capacity calculated from the basic solution of the large program. The industry averages, shown in Table 7-5 were reduced slightly to 82, 70, and 56 percent for Periods I to III, respectively. These values are the minimum operating constraints on all yards when the large volume of ship orders is to be redistributed evenly throughout the industry. For a less extensive work-dispersion policy, an appreciable difference in values (70, 55, 34 percent) could be found only by permitting the three most efficient yards to enter freely and subtracting their utilizations and capacity from the industry totals from which the minimum use quotas are figured. Finally, for the third alternative, minimum production rates of 30, 23, and 15 percent were chosen for the three periods.

Appendix J Estimating Steel Throughput Capacity

In addition to shipyard eligibility and experience, the question of shipyard capacity and its measurement frequently enters into establishing yard capability. Employment "loads" are usually used as proxies for measuring capacity, although admittedly these are imperfect, as is manufacturing value added, total revenue or sales, tonnage launched, and any other measure one can think of. A better, and perhaps more common, global measure of shipyard size or capacity, particularly in Europe and Japan, is steel tonnage throughput. Since foreign-built tankers and cargo ships have relatively little outfitting, i.e., are *steel*-intensive, steel throughput represents a fairly sound unit of measure for foreign yard capacity. In the United States, however, the product mix is much more heterogeneous, and steel throughput a much less perfect unit of measure. U.S. naval ships include more on-board equipment and involve more outfitting labor; thus, they are relatively more *labor*-intensive. Electronic equipment, armaments, and outfitting represent a far larger share of total costs in U.S. naval ships than in the large tankers and cargo ships now being built in Europe and Japan. Ideally, therefore, a truly universal measure of shipyard size or capacity would include not only steel throughput but some other unit measuring outfitting activities as well. To date, however, no such all-inclusive measure has been developed.

In order to gain some preliminary insight into the relative steel throughput capacity of U.S. shipyards, we estimated peaks of recent or future monthly steel throughputs for naval and commercial ship construction.[1] On the basis of these estimates, it was possible to rank shipyards in accordance with steel throughput capacity. The results are listed in Table J-1.

Table J-1
Estimated Peaks in Monthly Steel Throughput by 14 Yards in Naval and Commercial-Ship Construction, 1963 to 1970 (Ranked in Order by Naval and Commercial)

Shipyard*	Naval and Commercial (tons)	Naval Only (tons)	Applicable Dates Used for Estimate
Yard 2†	3,527	1,135.5	Feb.-Apr. 1968
			Jan.-Sept. 1968
Yard 3		563.3	Nov. 1966-Jan. 1968
	5,606		May-Aug. 1968
	6,394		Aug. 1968
Yard 4†	–	2,665	May 1968-Feb. 1969
Yard 5†	4,870	2,937	Apr.-Oct. 1968
Yard 6†	3,815.6		May-Sept. 1968
	3,605		Oct. 1963-Jan. 1964
		1,342	Oct. 1963-July 1964
Yard 7	–	1,450	March-July 1966
Yard 8†	–	1,698	May-July 1970
		1,805	July 1970
Yard 9	766	600	July 1967-May 1968
			Jan.-Oct. 1963
Yard 10	–	415	Dec. 1966-March 1967
Yard 11†	–	422	Dec. 1966-Apr. 1967
Yard 12	–	234	Aug. 1968-March 1969
Yard 13	–	305	Apr.-June 1968
Yard 14	–	485	Apr.-Sept. 1967
Yard 15†	2,708	‡	

*Yard 1 not applicable.

†Variations on either side of peaks weighted and averaged in.

No recent naval construction.

Bibliography

Bibliography

Shipbuilding Economics and Management

Bannerman, Graeme C. "Multi-Year Ship Procurement and Other Ship Acquisition Concepts." *Journal of ASNE*, December 1967.

Bosley, D.B. "The Secret to Japanese Shipbuilding Success." *Journal of ASNE* 79 (1967).

Couch, John C. "The Cost Savings of Multiple Ship Production." *SNAME* Great Lakes and Great Rivers Section, May 23, 1963. *International Shipbuilding Progress*, August 1963.

Eckhardt, W.H., and Jackson, H.A. "Some Modern Procedures for Shipyard Operation." *SNAME* New England Section, June 24, 1961.

Ernst and Ernst. "Report on Indirect Government Aids to U.S. and Foreign Maritime Industries." For Shipbuilders Council of America, Washington, D.C., April 1967.

Erwe, Eric. "European Shipbuilding Methods and Economics." *SNAME*, Joint California Sections Meeting, October 1961.

Fassett, F.G., Jr., ed. "The Shipbuilding Business in the United States of America." *SNAME*, 1948.

Ferguson, W.B. "Shipbuilding Costs and Production Methods." Cornell Maritime Press, 1944.

Frankel, E.G. "Aspects of Ship Manufacturing Requirements for Increased Productivity." *SNAME*, Metropolitan Section, April 1968.

Geddes, R.M., Chairman, OBE, "Shipbuilding Inquiry Committee 1965-1966 Report." Present to Parliament, March 1966.

Hoffman, L.C., and Tangerini, C.C. "Reducing Costs of American Ships." *Transactions SNAME*, vol. 69, 1961.

Hood, Edwin M., and Sonenshein, Nathan. "An Objective Look at Shipbuilding in the United States." Paper presented at *SNAME* Diamond Jubilee Meeting, June 1968.

Krietemeijer, J.H. "Standardization and Series Production in Shipbuilding." *Shipbuilding and Shipping Record*, February 16, 1968, pp. 225-227, 240.

Lane, F.C. "Ships for Victory: A History of Shipbuilding under the Maritime Commission in World War II." Baltimore: John Hopkins Press, 1951.

Lenaghan, J. "Present Trends in the Shipbuilding Industry." *Transactions RINA*, 1962.

Logistics Management Institute. "Life Cycle Costing in Equipment Procurement." Washington, D.C., April 1968.

Mack-Forlist, D.M. "Shipyard Management: The Operation of Man-Machine System." Paper presented at *SNAME* Diamond Jubilee Meeting, June 1968.

———. "United States Shipyards and the Effects of Disarmament." Report Submitted to Columbia University, 1964.

Motor Ship, "British Shipbuilding Costs: November 1967." Special Survey, "British Shipbuilding Today," November 1967, p. 63. *(BSRA Journal*, December 1967).

Muller, W.H. "Some Notes on the Design of Crew Accommodations for Merchant Vessels." *SNAME* New England Section, January 1958.

Parkinson, J.R. "The Economics of Shipbuilding in the United Kingdom." Cambridge University Press, 1960.

Patton, James, Chairman to the Joint Industry Committee, "Productivity and Research in Shipbuilding." Report to the Main Committee, Great Britain, February 1962.

Schultz, H.G. "The Influence of Frame Spacing Variation on the Cost of Mixed Frame Vessel." Institute of Engineering Research, University of California, Berkeley, May 1964.

Shinto, Dr. Hisashi, "Growth of the Japanese Shipbuilding Industry." *Shipping World and Shipbuilder*, October 1966.

———. "The Shipbuilding Industry in Japan after World War II." Annual Tanker Conference, American Petroleum Institute, May 1967.

Shipbuilders Council of America. "Report on Capacity and Utilization of Private Shipbuilding and Ship Repair Facilities, 1963." Washington, D.C., April 1964.

———. "The Prospects for Reducing U.S. Shipbuilding Costs." Washington, D.C., March 1966.

Shipbuilding and Shipping Record, "How Maritime Countries Support Shipping." November 23, 1967.

Steward, J.L. "The Role of the Accountant in a Shipyard," *Transactions*, Institute of Eng. & Shipbuilders in Scotland, 1965.

Webb Institute of Naval Architecture, Center for Maritime Studies. *Improving the Prospects for U.S. Shipbuilding*. 1969.

Williams, Harry, Wells, John D., Johnston, Elizabeth R., and Sanders, Edward G. "An Economic Analysis of U.S. Shipbuilding Costs." Report R-120, Institute for Defense Analyses, Economic and Political Studies Division, December, 1966.

Yamamoto, N. and Kihara, H. "Recent Developments in Management and Production Methods in Japanese Shipyards." Paper presented at *SNAME* Diamond Jubilee Meeting, June 1968.

Zein, Charles. "Ship Procurement: Isn't There a Better Way?" *SNAME* Philadelphia Section, October 21, 1966. Also *Marine Technology*, July 1967.

Ziedins, R. "An Attempt to Correlate Ship Construction Costs to the Complexity of the Structure." Institute of Engineering Research, University of California, Berkeley, April 1963.

Learning-curve Theory

Alchean, Armen. "Reliability of Progress Curves in Aircraft Production." Rand Corporation, 1950.

Alchian, A.A. "Reliability of Progress Functions in Airframe Production," *Econometrics*, vol. 31, no. 4, October 1963, pp. 679-693.

Andress, Frank J. "Learning Curve: As a Production Tool," *Harvard Business Review*, Jan.-Feb. 1954.

Arrow, K.J. "The Economic Implications of Learning by Doing." *Review of Economic Studies*, vol. 29, no. 80, April 1962, pp. 155-173.

Asher, Harold. "Cost Quantity Relationships in the Airframe Industry." Rand Corporation, 1956.

Bureau of Labor Statistics. "Productivity Changes in Selected Wartime Shipbuilding Programs." See Bureau's Bulletin 824, Wartime Employment, Production and Conditions of Work in Shipyards.

Conway, R.W., and Schultz, A., Jr. "The Manufacturing Progress Function." *Journal of Industrial Engineering*, vol. 10, no. 1, 1959.

Cole, Reno R. "Increasing Utilization of the Cost-quantity Relationship in Manufacturing." *Journal of Industrial Engineering.* May-June 1958, pp. 173-177.

Gallagher, Paul F. *Project Estimating by Engineering Methods.* New York: Haydon Book Company, 1965.

Garg, A., and Milliman, Pierce. "The Aircraft Progress Curve Modified for Design Changes." *The Journal of Industrial Engineering*, Jan.-Feb., 1961, pp. 23-27.

Hirsch, W. Z. "Manufacturing Progress Functions." *Review of Economics and Statistics*, vol. 34, May 1952.

———. "Firm Progress Ratios." *Econometrica*, vol. 24, April 1956, pp. 136-143.

Eisemann, D.M. "The Progress Curve Computer," Rand Corporation, Report P-1492, September 17, 1958.

Journal of Industrial Economics, "Learning Curve and Its Application to the Aircraft Industry," vol. 13, no. 2, 1965, pp. 122-128.

Keachie, E.C., and Fontana, R.J. "Effects of Learning Curve on Optimal Lot Size." *Management Science*, vol. 13, October 1966, pp. B-102–B-108.

Kottler, J.L. "The Learning Curve: A Case History in its Application." *The Journal of Industrial Engineering*, vol. 15, no. 4, July-August 1964.

Novick, David. "Use of Learning Curve." Rand Corporation, Report P-267, November 9, 1951.

Oi, W.Y. "The Neo-classical Foundations of Progress Functions." *Economic Journal*, September 1967, pp. 579-594.

Preston, L.E., and Keachie, E.C. "Cost Functions and Progress Functions: An Integration." *American Economic Review*, March 1964, pp. 100-106.

Rapping, L.A. "Learning and World War II Production Function." *The Review of Economics and Statistics*, vol. 47.

Stanford Research Institute. *An Improved Rational and Mathematical Explanation of the Progress Curve in Airframe Production.* August 1949, p. 5.

Sturmey, S.G. "Cost Curves and Pricing in Aircraft Production." *Economic Journal*, December 1964, pp. 954-982.

Williams, Paul F. "The Application of Manufacturing Improvement Curves in Multiple Product Industries." *The Journal of Industrial Engineering*, March-April 1961, p. 108.

Shipyard Layout and Facilities

Campbell, W.J. "Stepping Stones in Tank Barge Construction," *SNAME* South Eastern Section, January 29, 1966. (*BSRA Journal*, December 1966.)

Darowski, H. "Flow-Planning Model for the Production of Hull Components." *Schiffbautechnik*, vol. 16, August 1966. (*BSRA Journal*, November 1966.)

Dunn, Thomas P. "Computer Simulation Applied to Facility Design and Performance Evaluation." *SNAME* Chesapeake and Hampton Roads Sections, September 1968.

Fortune, "New Ways for the Shipyards." July 1967.

Holden, Donald. "Address." *Journal of ASNE*, April 1966, pp. 251-256.

Hurst, R. "Towards a Technology of Shipbuilding." *Transactions NEC I*, vol. 83, 1966-1967.

Maritime Reporter, "Vancouver Shipyard." July 1, 1967.

Schmidt, Alfred. "An Advanced Concept of Improved Shipbuilding Fabrication and Material Handling." *Marine Technology*, vol. 2, no. 2, April 1965.

Shimizu, K., and Suzisaki, Y. "Total Quality Control in Shipbuilding." Reprint from Nippon Kokan Technical Report–Overseas, September 1965. (*BSRA Journal*, April 1967.)

Numerical Methods, Lofting, Drafting

Astrup, N.C. "Designing Hulls with Plates of Single Curvature, i.e., Developable Surfaces." In Norwegian, Norwegian University of Technology, Ship Model Tank Publication No. 92, 1966. (*BSRA Journal*, November 1967.)

Berger, S.A., Webster, W.C., et al. "Mathematical Ship Lofting." *Journal of Ship Research*, vol. 10, December 1966, p. 203. (*BSRA Journal*, June 1967.)

Brayton, W.C. "Application of Numerical Control to Shipyard Production." *SNAME* Chesapeake Section, September 1966. Also *Marine Technology*, January 1968.

Gospodnetic, D. "Numerical Definition of Ships' Hulls by Means of Elastic Interpolation." N.R.C. Canada, Bulletin Division of Mechanical Engineering and National Aeronautics Establishment, No. 4, Oct. 1-Dec. 31, 1965. (*BSRA Journal*, May 1967.)

Kilgore, U. "Developable Hull Surfaces." In *Fishing Boats of the World*, Published by Food and Agriculture Organization of the U.N., Fishing News (Books) Ltd., London, 1967.

Moses, Fred, and Tonnessen, Arne. "Dynamic Programming for Computing Optimal Plate Dimensions in Some Ship Structures." *European Shipbuilding*, vol. 14, no. 4, 1967.

Nachtsheim, J.J., Romberg, B.W., and O'Brien, J.J. "Computer Aided Structural Detailing of Ships (CASDOS)." *SNAME* Proceedings of Spring Meeting, Montreal, July 1967.

"Numerical Methods Applied in Shipbuilding." Proceeding of Conference, Oslo, Norway, October 1963.

Rosenblatt, A. "Wider Horizons for Numerical Control." *Electronics*, June 26, 1967.

Shama, M., and Miller, N.S. "A Design Study of a Numerically Controlled Frame Bending Machine." *Transaction RINA*, 1965.

Symposium Notes, "Computers in the Marine Industry." *SNAME* New England Section, March 1967. (*BSRA Journal*, December 1967.)

Tranter, P.G. "The Revolution in Drawing and Lofting Techniques." Paper No. 14, Engineering Materials and Design Conference, London, September 1965. (*BSRA Journal*, December 1966.)

Ulrrohsen, Birre B. "Applications of Numerical Control to Flame Cutting Machines: The Essi-Autocon System," International Institute of Welding Annual Assembly, Paris, 1965.

Williams, A. "Future Design of Ship Lines by Use of Analogue and Digital Computers," Swed. State Shipbuilding Exp. Tank, Publication No. 59, 1966. (*BSRA Journal*, August 1967.)

Steel Welding and Fabrication Techniques

Abe, K., et al. "Application of One-Side Automatic Welding to Shipbuilding." *Journal Soc. Nav. Arch. Japan*, June 1966. (*BSRA Journal*, November 1966.)

"Tape Controlled Flame-Cutting Machine," *Automation*, vol. 2, May 1967, p. 11. (*BSRA Journal*, October 1967.)

Hirschberg, Dipl.-Ing. Hans. "Numerical Control of Large Co-ordinate Flame Cutting Machines." *Shipbuilding and Shipping Record*, May 3, 1968.

____. "Rationalization of Production by Using Large Flame-Cutting Installations." (in German) *Hansa*, vol. 104, p. 627, Special Issue in April, 1967. (*BSRA Journal*, November 1967.)

Kenderesi, J. "Notes on One-side Submerged-Arc Butt Welding in Shipbuilding and Tank Construction." *Schiff and Hafen*, vol. 18, January 1966. (*BSRA Journal*, February 1967.)

Koch, B., and Welding, J. "CO_2 Welding is Today a Qualified Process within Shipbuilding." December 1965. (*BSRA Journal*, October 1966.)

Loger, J. "Automatic Oxygen-Cutting in Shipbuilding." *Sond. et Tech Conn.*, November 1965. (*BSRA Journal*, May 1966.)

MacMillan, W.R. "Economics of Shotblasting." *Ship and Boat Builder*, vol. 19, November 1966. (*BSRA Journal*, January 1967.)

"How A Progressive Yard Meets Workload." *Marine Engineering*, vol. 72, August 1967, p. 65. (*BSRA Journal*, December 1967.)

Matsuyama, Yutake, et al. "Plate Sliding Type Automatic One Side Welding in Assembly State of Hull Construction." *Journal of Soc. Naval Architects of Japan*, vol. 120, 1966, p. 259.

McDonald, J.M. "Typical Sub-assembly Methods in Shipbuilding." *SNAME* New England Section, March 25, 1947.

"Study on Pickling Method I: Ultrasonic Pickling Method II HCL Spray Pickline Method," Mitsubishi MI *Technical Review*, September 1965. (*BSRA Journal*, August 1966.)

Otani, M. "Application of One-Side Automatic Welding in Japanese Shipyards," *Jap. Shipbuilding & Marine Engineering*, vol. 2, May 1967, p. 23. (*BSRA Journal*, November 1967.)

"Optimization of Welding Technology in Shipbuilding." *Schiffbautechnik*, March, May, June, 1966. (*BSRA Journal*, February 1967.)

"A Simple Semi-Automatic Welding Process Used Extensively in Japan." *Shipbuilding and Shipping Record*, August 1965. (*BSRA Journal*, April 1966.)

"Computer-Controlled Profile-Cutting Machine." *Shipbuilding and Shipping Record*, vol. 107, June 16, 1966. (*BSRA Journal*, April 1967.)

"Glasgow-built Press for U.S. Yard." *Shipbuilding and Shipping Record*, Sept. 7, 1967.

"Application of One-Side Automatic Welding to Shipbuilding." *Shipbuilding and Shipping Record*, June 1966.

"Power Staging Supersedes Scaffolding." *Shipbuilding and Shipping Record*, Nov. 2, 1967.

Sillifant, R.R. "Numerically Controlled Flame-Cutting Machines in Computer-Aided Ship Design and Construction." *Shipbuilding International*, vol. 10, June 1967, p. 4. (*BSRA Journal*, August 1967.)

"The Feasibility of Extending the Use of Non-Welded Devices in the Assembly of a Ship's Hull on the Berth." *Sudostroenie*, no. 10, October 1966.

"Shipyards and Welding Modernization." *Weld. Metal Fab.*, vol. 34, August 1966, p. 312. (*BSRA Journal*, May 1947.)

Developed by URAGA. "New Vertical Electro-Gas Automatic Welding Device." *Japan Shipping and Shipbuilding*, June 1966. (*BSRA Journal*, September 1966.)

Outfitting and Machinery Installation

Chambers, M., et al. "Network Analysis and Its Application to Shipbuilding." *Transactions RINA* 1965.

Goldsmith, Alexander. "Collection of Power Plant Studies." IIT Research Institute, Chicago, February 1967.

Kanauchi, T. "Advance Fitting-Out by Kure Zosen." *Japanese Shipping and Shipbuilding*, vol. 11, October 1966. (*BSRA Journal*, April 1967.)

Witt, M.J. "Flow production, the Installation of Pipe in Bundles and the Assembly Block Technique, in Conjunction with Layout Models, etc." *Schiffbautechnik*, Nov. 15, 1965. (*BSRA Journal*, January 1967.)

"New Automatic Hull Painting Device Introduced at N.K.K. Tsurumi Shipyard." *Zosen*, vol. 12, May 1967, p. 27. (*BSRA Journal*, August 1967.)

Notes

Notes

Preface

1. Before the era of so-called total-package procurement by the Navy, these items were referred to as government-furnished equipment.

Chapter 1
U.S. Shipbuilding Industry: Productivity and Markets

1. James R. McCaul, "The Shipbuilding Industry in the U.S.," in Webb Institute of Naval Architecture, *Improving the Prospects for U.S. Shipbuilding,* 1969. p. 11.

2. Labor productivity is defined as output per unit of labor input or, alternatively, labor input per unit of output. The latter ratio is commonly used in the shipbuilding industry and is adopted here.

3. The construction even of most merchant ships requires the appropriation of funds for the construction subsidy by Congress and approved of their use by the Maritime Administration.

4. See Appendix B of Williams et al, "An Economic Analysis of U.S. Naval Shipbuilding Costs," for the number of U.S. naval ship programs from 1961 to 1965.

5. A similar breakdown for all ships and boats procured from 1951 to 1965 appears in Appendix B of Williams et al.

6. Further devaluations of the dollar beyond those of early 1972 may make some U.S. shipyards competitive worldwide.

Chapter 2
Shipyards, Demand Levels, and Ship Categories

1. This program represents a continuation of the federal shipbuilding subsidy at the rate sponsored by the Johnson Administration.

2. See, incidentally, the forecast of dollar volume of ship construction for 1969 to 1975 by the Shipbuilders Council of America in its *Weekly Bulletin* no. 49, Thursday, Dec. 5, 1968.

3. This procedure enhances the accuracy of the input constraints; see Section 3-2.

4. Relatively low proportions of their labor inputs are devoted to the propulsion systems and somewhat more to hull and electronics. See Appendix C, H. Williams et al., "An Economic Analysis of U.S. Naval Shipbuilding Costs," p. 123.

Chapter 3
Factor Supplies, Productivity, and Investment

1. See Appendix F for a more detailed description of how these figures were used.

2. Planning estimates provided by the U.S. Department of Defense and the Maritime Administration are used for a specific yard of intermediate efficiency. See Appendix C for further information on preparation of labor data for the representative yard.

3. The details of how the investment function for each yard was determined are contained in Appendixes F, G, and H.

Chapter 4
The Estimation of Shipyard Cost Functions

1. Conventional wisdom asserts that firms actually tend to bid below marginal cost with the expectation of making up the loss by overcharging for design changes requested by the navy. Getting a first contract also gives a considerable advantage in bidding for any subsequent ships of the same type. Even if conventional wisdom is correct, however, it does not affect the analytical value of our assumption. All yards have the same opportunity to underbid on the first series of ships and the amount by which they can underbid will be determined by their costs. More efficient yards can bid lower than others but a limit is still set by the relation between their cost curve and how much they think they can overcharge for design changes. Also our assumption that the entire order for one ship type will go to a single yard (unless it exceeds the capacity of the yard) means there is no further bidding to build the same ship.

2. U.S. Department of Commerce, Maritime Administration, *Relative Costs of Shipbuilding in the Various Coastal Districts of the United States* (Washington, D.C., 1967), pp. 12-13.

3. Ibid., pp. 10-12.

4. The adjustment process can be illustrated with some simple algebra. Define the following variables:

M_i = materials cost for ship i
L_i = standardized first-ship labor cost for ship i
A_{ij} = labor-cost adjustment factor for ship i in yard j
L_{ij} = adjusted first-ship labor cost for ship i in yard j
T_{ij} = total first-ship variable cost of ship i in yard j
r_j = regional wage differential for yard j (1.0 = standard)
h_j = hull-labor productivity differential for yard j (1.0 = standard)
o_j = outfitting-labor productivity differential for yard j (1.0 = standard)
a_i = proportion of hull labor in ship i
$1-a_i$ = proportion of outfitting labor in ship i

The labor-cost adjustment factor is obtained by first weighting the productivity differentials and then multiplying by the regional wage differential:

$$A_{ij} = r_j[a_{ihj} + (1 - a_i)o_j]$$

This is applied to the standardized labor cost to get the adjusted labor cost:

$$L_{ij} = A_{ij}L_i$$

The total variable cost is the sum of the labor cost and the materials cost:

$$T_{ij} = M_i + L_{ij}$$

5. These cost figures are derived in the discussion of production functions in Appendix D.

Chapter 5
A Linear Programming Model of the U.S. Shipbuilding Industry

1. See Appendix A for a short, general discussion of linear programming and a mathematical description of the model of the shipbuilding industry.

2. This model also could be used to examine the impact of the sequence of the contract awards on the allocation and cost of specific programs. However, the tests would be awkward and time-consuming and therefore were omitted.

3. See Appendix I for a discussion of the manner in which capital cost can be converted to a stream of annual payments and the role of the rate of return.

Chapter 6
The Small Shipbuilding Program with Early Peaking

1. A dodecade is a 12-year period, *Webster's New International Dictionary of the English Language, Unabridged, Second Edition*, 1949.

2. U.S. Department of Commerce, Maritime Administration, *Relative Costs of Shipbuilding in the Various Coastal Districts of the United States* (Washington, D.C.: 1967), p. 16.

3. In the larger program, discussed in Chapter 7, which also includes orders for fast-development logistics ships (FDLs), the Litton yard shows a decisive advantage in construction of these ships.

4. For the critical volume as a function of cost differences, see Table E-1. For the theory on which calculations are based, see Appendix E. If progress rates are different between new and old techniques, new relationships can be calculated.

5. For a 96 percent cost-progress curve, an increase in the length of a run from one to eight ships reduces unit costs by 12 percent. A further increase to 64 ships is necessary to achieve another 12 percent cost reduction.

6. This means that $7.6 billion today, plus the earnings gained in the interim, would be sufficient to pay these costs as they are incurred. Discounting takes cognizance of the interim productivity of capital and is necessary in order to compare, on an equivalent basis, any two streams of costs occurring in different time patterns. (These costs exclude government-furnished equipment and do not encompass any aircraft carriers.)

Chapter 9
Contract Dispersal Policies

1. See Appendix I for discussion of how these policies are implemented in the linear programming model.

2. Ernst and Ernst, *Capacity and Utilization of Private Shipbuilding and Ship Repair Facilities* (Washington, D.C., 1966).

3. It is instructive to note that in January 1972 President Nixon announced the order of three Merchant Marine ships from a West coast yard at a cost of $54.6 million. This brought to $200 million the total value of contracts negotiated between the Maritime Administration and West coast shipbuilders during the previous 18 months. All contracts were for small numbers of ships. (See N.Y. Times January 5, 1972. p. 25.)

Chapter 11
Summary and Conclusions

1. These numbers encompass only shipyard receipts for new ship construction and exclude aircraft carriers.

Appendix A
A Linear Programming Model of the U.S. Shipbuilding Industry

1. The means of solving the problem is described in numerous books and articles, including Charnes and Cooper; G.B. Dantzig, *Linear Programming and Extensions* (Princeton: Princeton University Press, 1963); G. Hadley, *Linear Programming* (Reading, Mass.: Addison-Wesley, 1962); Saul I. Gass, *Linear Programming*, (New York: McGraw-Hill, 1958).

2. Remember throughout that the choice of which problem is the dual and which the primal is entirely arbitrary.

3. "Prices" are not necessarily measured in terms of dollars but more generally in terms of *numeraire*. The numeraire simply allows comparison and combination of different goods.

4. For a proof see David Gale, *The Theory of Linear Economic Models* (New York: McGraw-Hill, 1960), pp. 19-20.

5. See Chapter 4 and Appendix F for discussions of cost curves and investment, respectively.

6. See Appendix G for a more complete discussion of the derivation of the R_{jk} elements.

Appendix B
Costs, Labor Use, and Ways Requirement Data

1. These are described in Section 3-2, 3-3, and 4-2.

2. Prior to the era of "total-package procurement" by the Navy, these items were referred to as "government-furnished equipment."

3. Information on the fraction of cost attributable to government-furnished equipment was provided by the Naval Ship Systems Command. The breakdown of shipbuilders' cost was taken from data submitted in bids and, therefore, represents bit statements and not *ex-post* records of performance.

4. Labor and materials cost indices for steel vessel contracts are prepared by the U.S. Department of Labor, Bureau of Labor Statistics.

5. This terminology means that average cost falls by 7 percent with each doubling of the number of output units produced after the first unit. It would be more appropriately called a 7 percent progress function. For the form of the function, see Table B-2.

6. These coefficients, taken jointly, imply a rate of cost progress of about 96.5 percent for average variable shipyard cost (excluding overhead) and 97 percent for total shipyard cost (including overhead, for which no "progress" is claimed).

7. These factors for design and engineering were obtained as averages from shipyard bid statements.

8. This factor was obtained from an examination of shipyard employment data.

9. Business and Defense Services Agency, Industry Evaluation Board Summary Analysis No. 754 (May 3, 1967), Secret.

10. For data on this subject, See U.S. Department of the Navy, Naval Ship Systems Command, *Monthly Progress Report on Shipbuilding and Conversion.*

Appendix C
The Processing of Yard Employment Data

1. See U.S. Bureau of the Census, *1963 Census of Manufactures, Industry Statistics: Ship & Boat Building, Railroad and Miscellaneous Transportation Equipment*, (MC63(a)-37C (Washington, D.C.: U.S. Government Printing Office, 1966), p. 16.

Appendix D
Production Functions, Labor Supply, and the Costs of Output Expansion

1. James Dei Rossi and Willard W. Smith, *Price Indices for U.S. Shipbuilding*, Resource Management Corporation, RMC Research Document RD-002, (June 1967).

2. This value for the elasticity of labor supply was obtained by regressing monthly U.S. shipyard employment in hours on average real wages in shipbuilding, alternative wages in the construction industry, and the number of ships being built and on order during the year. Data for 1947 to 1966 were used. For employment and wage data by month, see U.S. Bureau of Labor Statistics, *Employment and Earnings Statistics for the United States, 1909-1967*, Bulletin 1312-5 (Washington, D.C.: U.S. Government Printing Office, 1967). For the number of ships building and on order, see Shipbuilders Council of America, *Annual Report, 1967*, Washington, D.C.

Appendix F
Yard Technology and Investment

1. By cancelling out L_{i1}, it is clear that

$$\frac{L_{i1}}{TL_1} \; \frac{L_{i2}}{L_{i1}} = \frac{L_{i2}}{TL_1},$$

where L_{ij} denotes labor inputs in subprocess i in yard j and TL_j denotes total hull-labor inputs in yard j. Moreover,

$$\sum_{i=1}^{n} \frac{L_{i1}}{TL_1} \; \frac{L_{i2}}{L_{i1}} = \frac{TL_2}{TL_1}.$$

Appendix G
Conversion of Lump-Sum Investment Costs to Periodic Rental Charges

1. If r equals 10 percent, A becomes

$$A = \frac{\$100{,}000 \times 0.10}{1-(1.10)^{-12}} = \frac{\$10{,}000}{0.6812} = \$14{,}700$$

2. A equals \$22,500. Since A was calculated from P equal to \$100,000, P_{12} must be equal to \$100,000. If r equals 20, then

$$\sum_{i=1}^{4} \frac{1}{(1 + r)^i} = 2.588 \quad \text{and} \quad 2.588 \times 22{,}500 = \$58{,}230$$

$$\sum_{i=1}^{8} \frac{1}{(1 + r)^i} = 3.837 \quad \text{and} \quad 3.837 \times 22{,}500 = \$86{,}332$$

Appendix H
Calculation of the Savings from Investment

1. The model contains the implicit assumption that investment is infinitely divisible. This is not so, for in reality it is "lumpy." However, if the solution of the program calls for the yard to invest at all in one group of equipment, it usually calls for it to invest to the limit permitted.

Appendix J
Estimating Steel Throughput Capacity

1. We used the following method of estimation:

From comprehensive data on Fiscal Year Programs, 1958 to 1968, we listed all ships built by the 14 shipyards included in the model. Next we obtained the hull weight for each ship. Then, using shipbuilding Progress Reports, we calculated the number of months from start of construction to launch for each naval ship. (Ways time only, i.e., keel to launch, was used for commercial ships, because, for these ships, generally only 5 percent of total production work is complete at keel laying.) Assuming a homogeneous distribution of steel work throughout the period of construction, we divided the hull weight by the number of months which yielded a value for average tons per month processed for each ship.

Finally, by plotting the duration of construction for all ships in a yard, it was possible to add up the average throughput for each month and thereby determine the peak. In certain instances where there was wide variation before and after the peak, we averaged these varying values with the peak value and weighted them by the number of months duration of each. A dagger appears in the table whenever averaging occurred.

Index